THE JEWISH VALUES SERIES

When a Jew celebrates

ILLUSTRATIONS BY ERIKA WEIHS

When a Jew celebrates

by **HARRY GERSH**

with Eugene B. Borowitz and Hyman Chanover

THE JEWISH VALUES SERIES

BEHRMAN HOUSE, INC. PUBLISHERS NEW YORK, N.Y.

For the teachers of our religious schools
—not forgetting Ruthie

Published by Behrman House, Inc.
1261 Broadway, New York, N.Y.

Library of Congress Catalog Card Number: 70-116678
Standard Book Number: 87441-091-6

Manufactured in the United States of America

DESIGNED BY BETTY BINNS

Contents

1 *Time* 9

Time and the individual

2 *Life begins* 17
3 *Naming* 27
4 *Bar Mitzvah, Bat Mitzvah, Confirmation* 35
5 *Marriage* 44
6 *The home and the family* 56
7 *Death* 67

Time and the community

THE WEEKS
8 *The Sabbath* 83
9 *Every day* 98

THE MONTHS

10 *The Jewish calendar* 105

THE SEASONS

11 *Spring: Passover* 117

12 *Spring into summer: the Omer* 132

13 *Summer: Shavuot* 140

14 *Fall: Sukkot* 150

15 *The cycle ends: Simḥat Torah* 161

THE SPECIAL DAYS

16 *Ḥanukkah* 171

17 *Tu bi-Shevat* 182

18 *Purim* 189

19 *Tisha be-Av* 199

THE YEARS

20 *The Days of Awe* 209

21 *Rosh Hashanah* 218

22 *Yom Kippur* 229

The goal of time

23 *The End of Days* 245

GLOSSARY OF HEBREW TERMS *251*

INDEX *254*

THE JEWISH VALUES SERIES

When a Jew celebrates

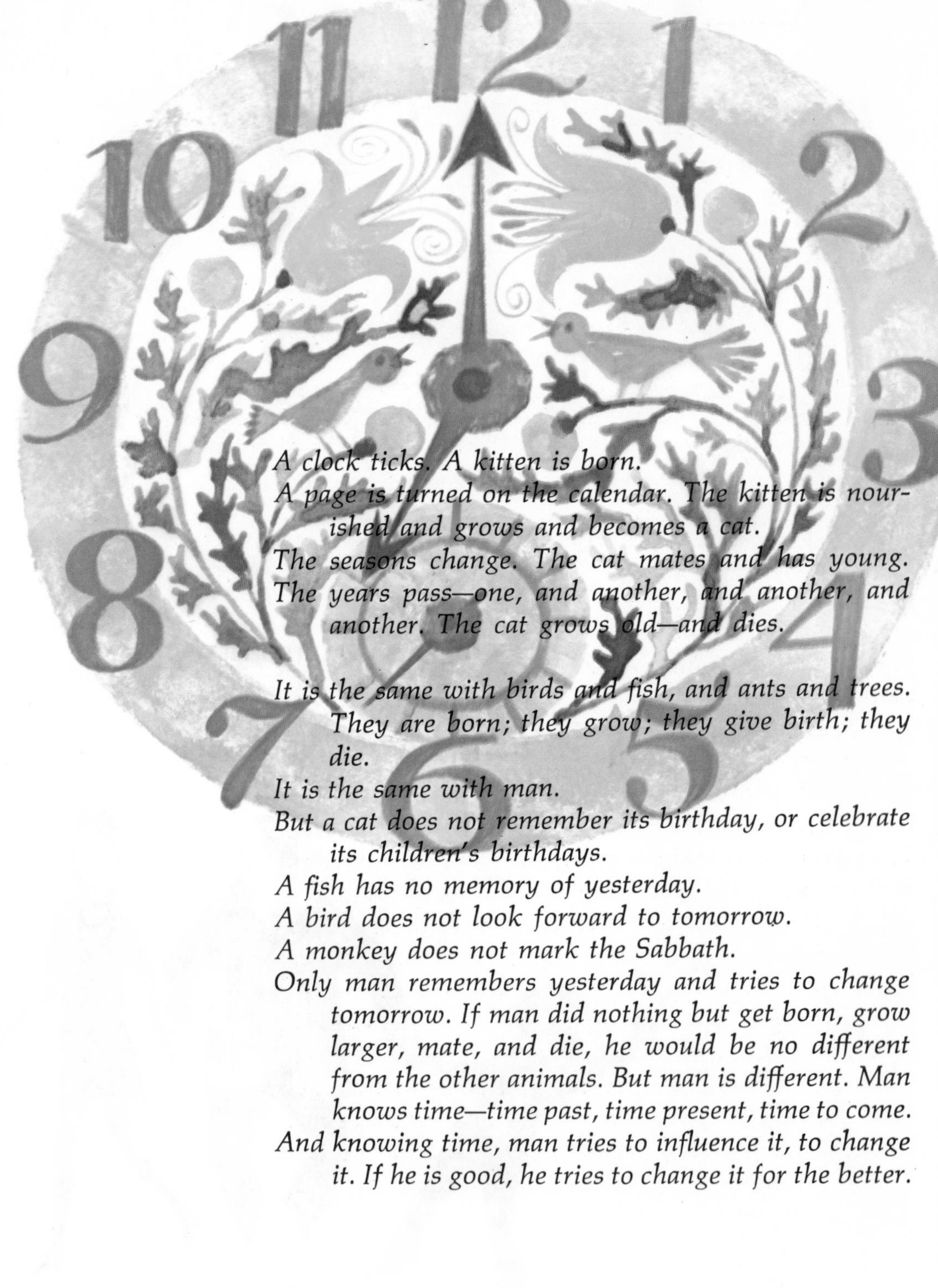

A clock ticks. A kitten is born.

A page is turned on the calendar. The kitten is nourished and grows and becomes a cat.

The seasons change. The cat mates and has young.

The years pass—one, and another, and another, and another. The cat grows old—and dies.

It is the same with birds and fish, and ants and trees. They are born; they grow; they give birth; they die.

It is the same with man.

But a cat does not remember its birthday, or celebrate its children's birthdays.

A fish has no memory of yesterday.

A bird does not look forward to tomorrow.

A monkey does not mark the Sabbath.

Only man remembers yesterday and tries to change tomorrow. If man did nothing but get born, grow larger, mate, and die, he would be no different from the other animals. But man is different. Man knows time—time past, time present, time to come.

And knowing time, man tries to influence it, to change it. If he is good, he tries to change it for the better.

1

Time

The goal of time

When did time begin? Our Rabbis said that time began before the creation of the moon and the stars, before God divided the heavens from the earth.

Will time end? According to the Jewish idea, time has a goal, a reason. Time exists so that man can grow better, and in growing better, make the world better. Time will reach its goal when everyone in the world is absolutely good, when every person will do only that which is absolutely fair and just, when there will be no hunger, no war, no injustice or meanness of any kind. Then, in a way, time will end. So Jews call this period the End of Days, or the Days of the Messiah, or the Kingdom of God.

To a Jew, this is the reason God gives us time and each person is expected to use his time to bring men closer to this goal of everlasting peace and justice. You can help bring the Days of the Messiah closer by living

TIME AND THE KINGDOM OF GOD

Time has a beginning and an end. It began long, long ago. It will end when the Kingdom of God has come. The story of the Jews began 3,800 years ago. Moses, David, Akiva, Maimonides, Herzl, and YOU are part of the ongoing story of the Jews. Jews still to come will be part of it. Working together, they and you help bring the Kingdom of God.

justly and mercifully, by being absolutely fair to all other beings on this earth. The Torah, with its rules of mercy and justice, was given to the Jews by God so that our whole people could build its life on Torah and move the world closer to the End of Days.

Our place in time

Time began millions of years before you were born. And time will continue for millions of years after you die. Yet in all this time, among all the billions of individuals, Jews believe that every single individual is important—that you are important to God. What you do with your time, how you spend your time, helps determine the world of the future.

This is easy to understand if you think of great men. Certainly Einstein changed the future of the world. Caesar and Napoleon changed the world. Moses and Johanan ben Zakkai changed the world; so did Theodor Herzl.

It's not so easy to understand how each person is important in time; but an old story explains it this way.

A nation was once conquered because its army lost an important battle. The battle was lost because the king of that nation did not arrive on the battlefield in time to rally his army. The king did not appear in time because he was thrown from his horse while galloping to the battle. The horse threw the king because it stumbled when it lost its shoe. The shoe was lost because a horseshoe nail was missing. The nail was missing because the blacksmith overslept and didn't have time to check the king's horse.

Who was to blame? The army? The king? The horse? The blacksmith? Everything and everyone counts.

There's a Jewish story with the same point. It was told by the Baal Shem Tov, the founder of Ḥasidism. There was plague in the city of a great king and none of the doctors of the city could cure it. One day the king saw a magic bird resting on the topmost tower of the castle. The king knew that this bird could cure the sickness in the city. He called the royal guard and ordered them to get it down. So they formed a human ladder, one man standing on the shoulders of the next, until the topmost man could almost reach the bird. Then one weakened, and they all fell.

"So it is with us," the Baal Shem Tov said. "The man of holiness depends on the support of other men to attain the summit of holiness and bring down God's love. But when one person weakens, the whole structure falls and the *Tzaddik* [the man of holiness] must begin again."

No one can take your place in time, in the world. No one can do what you yourself can do. You have no substitutes. You are utterly unique, completely different

YOU AND YOUR OWN TIME

Your time in this story is NOW. What you do with your time and how you use it are important. You can help shape your own time and time to come—you can make it better.

from every other living creature that ever existed or ever will exist.

You are the nail. Your family is the shoe. Your community is the horse. The Jewish people is the king. The nations of the world are the army. The future of mankind is at stake.

Where will you be at that moment in time when you —the nail—are needed for the shoe, for the horse, for the king, for the battle, for the nation?

You, too, will change the world in small ways or in large—and so you are important in time.

With each tick of the clock, with each turn of the calendar, you are building your own future—and the world's.

Changing rhythms

Time doesn't roll on like a flat, unending, unchanging road. Time has hills and valleys, left turns and right, smooth places and rough. There are periods of light and periods of dark; time when it is hot and time when it is cold.

These changes in time have a rhythm—the quick rhythm of days, the slower rhythm of months, the still slower rhythm of seasons, reappearing year after year.

With time, each person changes. And the changes of a person also have a rhythm: A child is born, walks, talks, knows. The youth becomes an adult, marries, has children of his own. The old person moves to a slower rhythm, declines physically, and dies.

Man remembers

The cat, bird, ant, fish, tree, all have their own rhythms in time. But man is unlike them because he thinks, he remembers, he hopes—and he celebrates. He knows the past and looks ahead to the future. He looks back to the great events of the past and remembers them with special ceremonies. He looks forward to each new season and welcomes it with rituals. He marks his own

MAN REMEMBERS AND CELEBRATES

Man remembers events and celebrates them. We celebrate the birthday of a child with a birthday party. We celebrate the birth of the New Year at Rosh Hashanah. We celebrate the beginning of understanding of the Torah with Bar or Bat Mitzvah. We celebrate God's giving the Torah at Shavuot. All through the year celebrations link a Jew to the Jewish people—and link the Jewish people to God.

birthday and marriage with festivities and remembers the deaths of his close ones and great ones with quiet and solemn acts. Man is the celebrating animal. His time is filled with holy days and anniversaries.

Just as each life has its birth and its birthdays, so each year has its Rosh Hashanah, its New Year celebration. Just as each year has its Simḥat Torah, so each life has its Bar or Bat Mitzvah.

Man celebrates

Time and memory cannot be separated.

If you could not remember your name, your parents, where you live, where you go to school, what has happened to you, you wouldn't be you. Time would be meaningless to you.

It's the same with peoples and nations. Their memories identify and separate them. Christians celebrate Christmas and Easter. Muslims mark the fast of Ramadan when their holy book was revealed.

So, too, does every Jew remember the Exodus from Egypt, the giving of the Torah, the destruction of the Temples, the good centuries and the bad since then.

It is this knowledge of ourselves—these memories—that make us Jews. If they were lost, our people would be lost. So we mark the great events in the lives of our people with celebrations and holidays and remembrance days. And even when we celebrate a private day, a birth, a Bar Mitzvah, a marriage, we link ourselves to our people by celebrating our joy their way.

We also link ourselves and our time to God. Put another way: We are not alone in time. God is always with us. The rhythm of time—sunup and sundown, moon rising and moon going down, winter, spring, summer, fall—is God's. The rhythm of life—birth, circumcision, Bar and Bat Mitzvah, marriage, death—is God's. So we want God to be present in the way we mark these days—and so present in our thoughts. Then we know our lives and the lives of all the Jews will help bring the Days of the Messiah.

One of our old Jewish books, the Zohar, explains it like this: "Whenever the Jews on earth rejoice in their

MAN LOOKS AHEAD

Man thinks and plans. He considers how best to use his time. Celebrations and holidays help us to remember, help us to think about what is important in life—and to plan ahead.

festivals, they give praise to the Lord. They put on fine clothes, and pile their tables with good food. So the angels ask, 'Why do the Jews pamper themselves so much?' And God answers, 'They have a distinguished Guest today. I am with them.' "

Time and the individual

Make believe today is your birthday.
To every one else, it is just another day.
But not to you.
To you, today is a very special day.

You have many special days.
So does your family.
You—and your family—will have many more:
Bar Mitzvah or Bat Mitzvah, Confirmation, marriage—
and many more.

They are the special days of your time.
It is almost as if you had a special calendar
in which the red-letter days are different
from all others.

Let us talk about your life.
About your time,
And how you and other Jews will celebrate it.

2

Life begins

The miracle of birth

The days of Biblical miracles are long past. The sea does not divide for us, and the blast of the shofar does not shatter the walls of a city. But the greatest miracle occurs a thousand times every day. The miracle of birth.

Birth is a double miracle for Jews. First is the miracle of life itself, the creation of a new human being. Second, although this miracle has occurred billions of times in the past, each birth brings forth a totally new, totally different individual.

The Talmud teaches: "Man stamps many coins from the same mold, and every coin is exactly the same. But God has stamped many people from the same mold [the mold of Adam], yet not one is like his fellow man. Therefore, one must say, 'For my sake was the world created.' "

Animals conceive and give birth to young in much

BIRTH

The birth of a baby is a miracle of creation. It is a time of joy for the parents and for the Jewish people. So we celebrate and give thanks to God at home and in the synagogue.

the same way as human beings. But there is a very important difference between man and animal in the creation of young. Animals conceive their young because some instinct tells them to. They do so without understanding or thought.

Man chooses to have babies. He does it knowingly, purposefully. So when what he has planned comes about, when the miracle he wanted occurs, he is very happy.

The family is filled with great joy. Father and mother have become one through the child which they conceived together. Together, they have created a new being; together, they have repeated the act of creation. But since creation is a Godlike act, Jews say that a child really has three parents: mother, father, and God.

Children of promise

The birth of a Jewish child is not only a time of joy for the parents; it is shared by all Jews. Every Jewish child is a promise for the Jewish people. A Jewish child will carry into the future the message and the work of his people and its Prophets and Rabbis. A Jewish child is a guarantee of the Jewish future.

A legend says:

When God was about to give the Torah to Israel, He asked them, "Will you accept My Torah?" And they answered, "We will!"

God said, "What guarantee will you give Me that you will follow My Law?" The Jews offered the Fathers—Abraham, Isaac,

Jacob—as their pledges. But God said that the Fathers sometimes had lacked faith.

Then Israel said, "We offer our Prophets as pledges." But God said that the Prophets had sometimes sinned.

Then Israel said, "Our children will be our guarantees that we will follow the Torah." And God said, "If you pledge that your children will follow Me, such a pledge I do indeed accept." And He gave the Torah to the Jews.

Ceremonies and celebrations

All the Jewish celebrations, all the joyous days, involve three things in one way or another. There is a feast. There is the family. There are ceremonies. Since it is a happy time, we will want to have a fine meal to celebrate it; at the least a special snack. Sometimes there are special foods, sometimes just a special mood. But for us, to rejoice means to eat together in happiness. Not alone. We want the whole family there. Mother and father, grandmothers and grandfathers, brothers and sisters—and if it is a big celebration, uncles and aunts and cousins, too. In fact, when we celebrate we celebrate with the Jewish community. They are not merely our people but sort of our family spread very wide. And there are always ceremonies, candles and wine, blessings and prayers. For we are not alone in time. We are linked with God in our lives and in the life of our people. We celebrate His being with us now and His having made the celebration possible for us. Sometimes we are in the synagogue. Sometimes at home. It makes no difference. We want Him with us; we want to be with Him. So in our joy on a special day we say:

בָּרוּךְ אַתָּה יְיָ. אֱלֹהֵינוּ מֶלֶךְ הָעוֹלָם. שֶׁהֶחֱיָנוּ. וְקִיְּמָנוּ.
וְהִגִּיעָנוּ לַזְּמַן הַזֶּה:

Blessed art Thou, Lord our God, King of the universe, who has kept us alive and given us strength and made it possible for us to reach this happy day.

PLEDGE AND COVENANT

Israel gave its children as pledges to God for the Torah. They share in Israel's Covenant with God.

This is the *Sheheḥeyanu* blessing, and it will occur many times in your life.

Sign of the covenant

The most important ceremony marking the birth of a Jewish boy is circumcision.

On the eighth day after birth, Jewish boys are circumcised. According to the Torah, this began with Abraham. Since then, a man cannot be considered a Jew without circumcision.

All great or important events have physical symbols. A marriage is marked by a wedding ring. The victory of the Maccabees is marked by the Ḥanukkah menorah. The greatest thing in the life of the Jews, the covenant between God and Israel, is marked by circumcision. It is the sign of the agreement between God and the Jewish people to care for one another—the Jews to love God and follow His Torah, God to love the Jews and help them.

Why did this minor operation become the symbol of the covenant? We do not really know. We only know that it was practiced by many peoples at the time of

Abraham. Many peoples still practice it. All Muslim boys are circumcised, as is the custom of many peoples in the East. Though Christians do not believe in circumcision as a religious rite, they sometimes practice it as a health measure.

That explanation is very old. The Greek historian, Herodotus, 2,500 years ago, mentions it. Today we know that certain diseases are rare among circumcised people. Some scholars think circumcision was a mark of identification, just as primitive tribes use tattoos or specially shaped scars. But these are guesses. They do not come near explaining the great importance Jews give circumcision.

We do know that the Jews made circumcision a special Jewish *mitzvah,* commandment. Just as the Jews took ancient harvest festivals and gave them special Jewish religious meaning, so they adopted the ancient custom of circumcision and made it the special mark of the Jew.

מִצְוָה

Nor have the Jews ever doubted its importance. In many times and places it has meant death to be a Jew. Yet this very obvious sign of Jewishness—circumcision —was never rejected.

Even today, among Jews who have given up some —or all—of the other Jewish rites and ceremonies, this sign of Jewishness is kept. These Jews may eat bread during Pesaḥ; they may not go to synagogue. But they do circumcise their male children.

THIS HAPPY DAY

We celebrate happy days with feasts and family gatherings and ceremonies, with candles and wine, blessings and prayers. We celebrate in the synagogue, we celebrate at home.

The Berit Milah

The ceremony of circumcision is called *Berit Milah*—*berit,* meaning "covenant"; *milah,* meaning "circumcision." According to tradition, it must take place on the eighth day after birth unless the child is too weak. It is so important that even if the eighth day falls on the Sabbath or Yom Kippur, the Berit Milah is still held. Circumcision may be done in the hospital, in the synagogue, or at home. Today many parents prefer to have the circumcision done in the hospital. That has recently led to complications because mothers and their new babies often leave the hospital before the eighth day. In such cases, the circumcision is done at home. However, some Jews have it done on any day before the baby leaves the hospital.

Circumcision is a minor operation. It is done by a man trained in this operation—called a *Mohel.* In the hospital the circumcision is sometimes done by a Jewish surgeon, with a rabbi there.

A formal Berit Milah ceremony involves many people, but there are four who are most important—in addition to the baby. Three people are there in person; one is there in spirit. The three real people are the godmother, the godfather, and the Mohel. The one who is there in spirit is the prophet Elijah. In fact, at a traditional Berit Milah ceremony there is an empty chair—for Elijah.

In such a traditional circumcision the godmother brings the baby into the room and hands him to the Mohel, who places him on the godfather's lap while the circumcision is performed. In most modern circumcisions, and in hospitals, of course, the baby is put on a table covered with a sterile sheet.

The ceremony opens with the Mohel reciting a blessing. Whenever a commandment is to be performed a

BERIT MILAH

Circumcision is a great mitzvah. It is the sign of the Covenant between the Jews and God. The prophet Elijah is the unseen guest at this ceremony of blessings and joy.

blessing is said before doing it. All such blessings have the same form. They begin with the usual praise and thanks to God:

בָּרוּךְ אַתָּה יְיָ. אֱלֹהֵינוּ מֶלֶךְ הָעוֹלָם:

Blessed art Thou, Lord our God, King of the universe.

Then they mention His giving us commandments:

אֲשֶׁר קִדְּשָׁנוּ בְּמִצְוֹתָיו. וְצִוָּנוּ . . .

who has made us holy through His commandments and commanded us . . .

And then we fill in the proper words. Here they are simply:

עַל־הַמִּילָה:

about circumcision.

As soon as the operation is completed, the father recites the prayer thanking God for commanding us "to initiate our sons into the Covenant of Abraham, our father." Then the father recites the Sheheḥeyanu. The men attending the ceremony then say: "Even as he has now been led to the covenant, so may this child be led in due time to study, to marriage, and to good deeds." The Mohel says a blessing over the wine, drinks a little, and puts a few drops on the baby's lips.

Then, as at all joyous events, the party begins.

The presence of Elijah

And what was Elijah doing there? There's a legend that Elijah once complained to God that the Jews were not following the Law. So God said Elijah must attend every circumcision from that time on so that "the voice that testified that Israel had forsaken the covenant must now testify that they are keeping the covenant."

There's another story: Elijah will announce the coming of the Messiah. But the Messiah could be any Jewish child. So Elijah has to be present at every circumcision to honor the one who will lead the world to justice, mercy, peace, and plenty.

Circumcision is unlike other mitzvot. There are many opportunities throughout life to practice the other mitzvot. Even if a Jew fails to keep the Sabbath one week, he can keep it all the other weeks. If he forgets to practice charity today, he can double it tomorrow.

The opportunity to keep the commandment of circumcision comes only once in a lifetime. And having been circumcised, a boy maintains that tie between the past and the future until the day of his death.

Circumcision is also very important to the parents. As the father became part of the people of the covenant by this sign, so his son follows him, and another tie binds them together. Through this new member of the Congregation of Israel the parents bind themselves closer to the great past of their ancestors.

It is important, too, to the grandfathers and grandmothers, to the uncles and aunts, to the cousins and second cousins everywhere. It means something to the whole community of Jews throughout the world. The ceremony and the prayers at this Berit Milah were heard at their Berit Milah, and at every Berit Milah a thousand, two thousand years ago. Every new circumcision is a sign that they will be heard a thousand years in the future. Or as long as it takes to bring the Days of the Messiah.

You can see why the Talmud says that the mitzvah of circumcision is as great as all other mitzvot combined.

Another ceremony marks the birth of a first-born son (the first-born son of the mother, not the first-born son of the father if he was married before). It too goes back to the Torah and is called *Pidyon ha-Ben*—"the redemption of the first-born."

PIDYON HA-BEN

Jews give thanks to God for all gifts, especially their children. The first of all good things, including children, is to be offered to God. The first-born son is redeemed from special service by a money gift.

Redeeming the first-born

Because all things come from God, the Bible says that all first-born things should be given Him as thanks for all that is to come. So the first fruits and first grains were brought to God. So, in a way, the first-born son belonged to God. But it became the custom for the father to give money to the Temple in place of his son. The father went to the Temple and gave the priests five *shekalim,* special coins used for such contributions at the Temple.

This ancient ceremony is continued among many Jews today even though the Temple in Jerusalem no longer exists. On the thirtieth day after the birth of a first son, a Kohen (one descended from the family of priests) is invited to the home—along with friends and relatives. The father gives the Kohen five shekalim (usually $5), and so the child is redeemed from special service to God. The Kohen usually gives this money to charity.

Coming into time is too important not to be noticed. It is important to the child to begin life with a sense of being part of a family, a people, a relationship with God. It is important to his family, for this marks a great step in their way through time. It is important to the Jewish people which sees that it will go on serving God through this baby. It is important to God who wants men to love and serve Him.

No wonder we are happy and celebrate as only men can!

3

Naming

You and your name

Jews believe that every person is different from every other person who ever lived. Each has a different history; each has a different set of feelings.

When people look at you, they see only the outside; how tall you are, the color of your hair and eyes. Someone who does not know you might identify you as "that kid."

"That kid" could be anyone. But you are not anyone. You are you, the unique individual. So to people who know you as an individual, you are David or Gail or Jonathan or Rachel.

One important difference between you and any other girl or boy is in your name. Your name identifies you as you. Your name is the most personal thing added to you from outside yourself.

Your name not only identifies you, it identifies your family. It may even identify your larger family—your

YOUR NAME

Your name stands for you. It stands for you alone, for you as a member of your family, and for you as a member of the Jewish people.

my name is:

people. Patrick Kelly is probably the son of Irish parents. Rosa Antonini likely has Italian parents. If your name is David Cohen, there will be little doubt about your ancestry.

So names are more than labels. They are you, and your parents, and your grandparents, sometimes going back into ancient history. They are an identification—and they are a responsibility.

Names are so important that the Talmud says the Jews were delivered from Egypt because they did not change their names. That is, their names helped them remain Jews; they did not become Egyptians.

What you do with your name—whether people will remember good things or bad when they hear your name—depends on what you make of yourself. Some names, like Lincoln, are remembered as a blessing; some, like Hitler, as a curse.

Rabbi Simeon said: "There are three crowns: being a priest; being a king; being a scholar of the Torah. But the crown of a good name is greater than all three." We cannot all be born priests or kings, or become scholars. But anyone can crown himself with a good name.

How do we get our names?

Names for boys and girls

At the circumcision of a baby boy, the Mohel announces the name of the child. Usually on the first Sabbath after the birth of a baby girl, the father is called up to the pulpit to pronounce the blessings over the reading of the Torah. The reader recites a prayer for his family and there he mentions the new baby's name.

Reform Jews have developed a somewhat different ceremony for naming girls. It generally takes place at a Friday evening service in the synagogue, some weeks after the baby is born so the mother can be present at the naming. At an appropriate place in the service, the rabbi recites a special prayer, like this one:

Our God, we thank You for all the blessings You bring us. Tonight we are especially happy because a daughter has been born to these parents. They stand together at this altar, praying that You may help them always to be wise and good parents, and that, in their love for their child, they may rear her to become a fine Jewess.

And now, here in this temple, and in the presence of this congregation, we give this child the English name of ——— and the Hebrew name of ———. May she grow up, O God, under Your protection, in good health and happiness, and may her life always bring joy to her parents and loved ones, to all Jews, and to the whole world, Amen.

NAMING CEREMONIES

The Mohel announces the baby boy's name at the Berit Milah. The rabbi announces the baby girl's name, at a synagogue service.

The names pronounced at these events are chosen by the parents of the new baby. How do they decide?

Choosing a name

Names were very important to the Hebrews in Bible times. The Bible says that every beast was paraded before Adam to see what name he would give to each animal.

Biblical names often describe something:

Names about the person himself: *Laban* means "white"; *Koraḥ* means "bald."

Names about what the person resembles: *Susan* means "rose"; *Jonah* means "dove"; *Tamar* means "palm."

Names about events in the life of the person: *Moses* means "he was drawn" (out of the water); *Isaac* means "he will laugh."

Names having to do with God: *Isaiah* means "may God save"; *Emanuel* means "God is with us"; *Elijah* means "the Lord is my God."

In Bible times a name belonged to a single individual and was not used after he died. There is only one Moses in the Bible, only one Abraham. There were twenty-one kings descended from David, but not one of the twenty-one names is repeated, and none is called David.

After the destruction of the First Temple (586 B.C.E.), when the Jews were taken in captivity to Babylon, names began to be repeated. Among the High Priests of the Second Temple (fifth century B.C.E. to first cen-

CHOOSING A NAME

Names are chosen for many reasons. A Jewish child may have both a Jewish and a secular name. Both names must be kept shiny.

tury C.E.) the names Simon, Johanan, and Onias were repeated many times. For five hundred years after the death of the great Hillel his family used only four names over and over again: Hillel, Simon, Gamliel, and Judah.

Sephardic Jews—those in the East and those originally from Spain—continue to name their children after living relatives—though seldom after a living parent. They see this as a mark of respect, as if they were saying, "We want the child to be like you."

Ashkenazic Jews—those in the West and those originally from Eastern Europe—on the other hand, will almost never name a child after a living person. For them naming is an honor to the dead, not the living.

There is no religious law in this; it is only custom. But custom in Judaism can sometimes be as strong as law.

Jewish names and secular names

Jewish children are usually given two names, a Jewish name and a name in the language of the country in which the family lives, a *secular* name.

This is not a new practice. When Palestine belonged to the Syrian Greeks, many Jewish leaders had both Jewish and Greek names, such as Tarphon, Symachus, Antigonus.

For a while, Jews simply translated their Hebrew names into the general language to get their secular names. *Baruch*, which means "blessed" in Hebrew, became *Benedict*, which means "blessed" in Latin. In Eastern Europe, where the everyday language was Yiddish, one might have the double names *Zvi-Hirsh*, or *Dov-Baer*. *Zvi* is "deer" in Hebrew, *Hirsh* is "deer" in Yiddish; *Dov* is "bear" in Hebrew, *Baer* is "bear" in Yiddish.

Today, many Jewish families use the first letter of the Hebrew name in choosing a secular name. Like so many customs no one knows where it started or why. But if a girl's Hebrew name is Sarah, her secular name might be Sally or Shelly. If a boy's Hebrew name is Abraham, his secular name might be Alfred or Arthur.

Jewish names were not limited to the Bible. In the Middle Ages a child born on a holiday might be named Yom Tov. Pesaḥ and Ḥanok (Ḥanukkah) were also names given to boys born during these holidays. A child born on Tisha be-Av might be called *Menahem*, the "comforter," a word used in the Biblical portion read on that fast day.

Today, many Jews have gone back to the Bible names. David, Jonathan, Esther, Sarah, Abigail, Daniel, Joshua, Joel, are all widely used.

"Son of" names

Throughout most of their history, Jews did not use second names. A child was identified as the son or daughter of his or her father: Johanan ben Zakkai. *Ben* is the Hebrew word meaning "son," *bar* is the Aramaic word, as in Bar Kokhba; and *ibn* is Arabic, as in Solomon ibn Gabirol.

Calling a child by his father's name was common to almost all peoples.

In Scotland and Ireland, *Mac* and *Mc* mean "son of," so *MacDonald* means "son of Donald." The *O* beginning used in Irish names generally means grandson, so *O'Hara* means "grandson of Hara."

In Wales a final, possessive *s* is added to the father's name. David son of John became David John's, and John's later became Jones.

Germans use son, spelled *sohn*—from which we get *Mendelssohn*, "son of Mendel."

Greeks use *ides*—*Moses Maimonides* is the same as "Moses ben Maimon."

The Slavic peoples (in Russia and Poland) use *vitch, witz, sky*, and *ov* for "son." Thus Davidov, Davidovitch, Davidowitz and Davidovsky, all mean "son of David."

Second names

In the eighteenth and nineteenth centuries, second names became common in Europe and the Jews were ordered to follow this practice. The first such law was issued in 1787 in Austria. Napoleon gave such an order in 1808; Prussia passed its law in 1812; Poland in 1821; Russia in 1844.

Some Jews were permitted to take their father's or family names—Abramson, Davidson, Cohen, Levy. Others took trade names: Schneider (tailor), Goldschmidt (goldsmith), Malamud (teacher). Or from the places where they lived: Berliner, Englander, Polack, Warshauer. Or colors: Schwartz (black), Roth (red), Weiss (white), Gelb (yellow), Braun (brown).

In some places, officials demanded bribes for pleasant-sounding names, like Greenberg (green mountain), or Silberstein (silver stone). If they didn't get money they gave names like Ferd (horse), Fresser (glutton), Eselkopf (donkey's head).

What's in a name?

Names are strange. We do not get our choice of names. Our first name is a gift from our parents, our second name is our family's name, which may have come by accident or the whim of some official. So the most important thing is what we do with our names.

Goldberg (gold mountain) used to be the name comedians used when they wanted to identify a funny Jew. But now Goldberg recalls a former Justice of the Supreme Court and Ambassador to the United Nations.

Einstein (one stone) is meaningless in itself; but all the world knows Albert Einstein.

What will your name mean to the people that know it?

Most of us have names that come from great men

SHEM TOV

You make your name a good name, a Shem Tov, by the way you live, the way you spend your time of NOW.

and women of the Bible or Jewish history, names carried by our grandparents or great-grandparents whom our parents admired and respected. These names were given to us in the hope that we would have the courage and strength and dedication of those great ancestors. All Davids cannot have the greatness of King David. All Deborahs cannot be leaders. But we can try to live up to what our family and our people believe we ought to be.

שֵׁם טוֹב

And we can bring honor to the name our parents gave us—and leave for another Jewish child a *Shem Tov*—a good name. If we do, we will have used our time, our years, to fulfill our people's dream: to make a world of love and understanding, to bring the Days of the Messiah.

4

Bar Mitzvah, Bat Mitzvah, Confirmation

What is evil?

Nothing in creation is evil in itself.

The hand of man can kill. But it is not evil. The hand of man can also create lasting beauty.

A wild animal kills. But it is not evil. Most animals kill only for food or to protect their young.

Atomic power could kill all mankind. But it is not evil. Atomic power also promises to provide water in the desert and food for the world's hungry.

Evil comes from the misuse of the gifts given to us. It comes most often from lack of knowledge and understanding. From ignorance comes fear, from fear comes evil. Evil begins in the darkness in man's mind.

But how do we know what is evil? How do we know the difference between evil and good? And how do we avoid evil?

We avoid evil by learning what is good; by learning to understand the ways of man and the ways of God.

Duty to study

That is why, to a Jew, it is a religious duty to study—particularly to study those things that give you understanding and so make you a better person.

This kind of study is so important to Jews that we consider it a form of worship. To study the Torah—and the other great books of the Jews which teach us the rules for a good life—is to reach for understanding.

That's why our Rabbis said: "It is permitted to change a House of Prayer into a House of Study; that is moving upward. It is not permitted to change a House of Study into a House of Prayer." (Of course, today both are found in one synagogue.)

On one occasion, says the Talmud, a group of Rabbis came to a city of Israel and asked for the guardians of the city. So the city councilors were brought. The Rabbis said, "These are not the guardians of the city." The citizens then asked, "Who are the guardians?" And the Rabbis said, "The scholars and teachers of the young, they are the guardians of the city."

A tradition of study

The heroes of most nations are warriors: Alexander the Great, Caesar, Richard the Lion-Hearted. Jews, too, have warrior heroes like the Maccabees, but their greatest men are heroes of the mind and of the spirit: Moses, Micah, Akiva, Maimonides, the Baal Shem Tov, Moses Mendelssohn. Why have you heard those names before even though you are young? Because

they are the sort of people Jews want their children to know about and follow.

One reason we believe the Jews have lived on when other peoples, in similar situations, died out, is because of this tradition of study. Each generation was able to pass on to the next the Torah and the law, the stories and ideas of all the great Jews who went before. They led the Jews, year after year, to knowledge of God and His way—and they preserved the Jewish people for thousands of years.

Celebrating learning

Jews have always been proud and happy when their children began to learn, and so they celebrated each big forward step in learning.

The first celebration comes when the child first goes to school. There was an old and very warm Jewish custom for this. Cutout Hebrew letters were smeared

A LIVING TRADITION

Study and knowledge, learning and Torah, are a living tradition for Jews. Learning is sweet. Jews celebrate their children's steps in learning, a child's first day at school, his entrance into Hebrew school, as holidays.

"COMING OF AGE"

Bar Mitzvah, or Bat Mitzvah, is a joyous celebration. It means that the young person has grown up enough and learned enough about Torah to be responsible for his own acts. That makes one truly a son or daughter of the Commandments.

with honey, which the five-year-old licked before leaving for school. Or letters were written on a small slate and the border was smeared with honey. It was a sweet introduction to the letters, the start of sweet memories of learning. In other places the custom was to bake cakes in the form of Hebrew letters which were given children on their first day in school. No matter what was done, starting school was a special day for the whole family and a time of special treats.

Many American congregations have a special consecration service for new students entering religious school. It is often part of the Simḥat Torah service. The young children march up to the *Bimah,* they stand before the Ark, and the rabbi welcomes them into the company of scholars. They may all then say the Shema and the rabbi will give them a blessing. Often they will get a small gift or certificate from the whole congregation, which is happy that they are entering a Jewish school.

Everyone has a bigger celebration when he finishes a period of learning—on graduation—than when he begins. This is true of the Jews, too. And for Jewish learning, the first big step—the first graduation—is the Bar and Bat Mitzvah.

Bar and Bat Mitzvah

ר מִצְוָה

ת מִצְוָה

Just as *bar* is the word for "son," *bat* is the word for "daughter." *Mitzvah* is "commandment." So "*Bar Mitzvah*" is "Son of the Commandments," and *Bat Mitzvah* is "Daughter of the Commandments."

According to the Mishnah, the book of laws put together about 200 C.E., every male Jew is *Bar Mitzvah* at 13.

Why 13? Why not 11, or 16, or 18—or 20?

Bar Mitzvah is much like citizenship. You are born a citizen of the United States, or of Canada. In much the same way you are a Jew the moment you are born.

But you cannot vote—even though you are a citizen—until you are 18 or 21 years old. In the same way, you are not a full, responsible citizen of the Jewish community until you have reached Bar or Bat Mitzvah at the age of 13. Until a child reaches age 13 he is still learning the difference between right and wrong, between good and evil. The child is also learning to control his actions, so that he will have the strength to do what is right and not do what is wrong. From then on, a child is supposed to have learned enough about himself and what is expected of him—to be responsible for his own acts—for the rest of his life.

That is what Bar Mitzvah means: The child has learned enough about the way of righteousness to become responsible for following it.

The Bar Mitzvah ceremony

The ceremony connected with becoming a Bar Mitzvah is a fairly new one. The Bible says nothing about Bar Mitzvah, and the Talmud very little. A boy came to services with his father and was called up to the Torah. That marked his Bar Mitzvah.

But during the Middle Ages in Europe it was the custom that boys under 13 were not permitted to put on *Tefillin* and were not to be called to read the Torah at services. Only when he reached 13 and could show that he understood their real meaning was the young man given these privileges. And that made it seem like the right time for a Jewish celebration.

After the synagogue ceremony, the boy's family and friends went to his home for a feast. At this party, the new Bar Mitzvah gave a speech in which he showed that he had studied the Torah and was a proper Bar Mitzvah. The Bar Mitzvah speech many boys now give is a reminder of that lecture on the Torah.

The Bar and Bat Mitzvah feast is not a special birthday party. It is a religious celebration. It is happy and gay like a party because the boy and his family and the whole Jewish community are joyful and delighted that he has come to full religious citizenship.

Being Bar or Bat Mitzvah is not something for only one day, or one year. The boy has become Bar Mitzvah for the rest of his life. A man of 70 is as much a Bar Mitzvah as a young man on his 13th birthday.

This is most important to remember: Bar Mitzvah is not a party; it is not even a ceremony at the synagogue; it is not something that happens once. Bar Mitzvah is a condition of life—and lasts all life long.

In the life of a girl, marriage is the most important religious event. She generally thinks of her wedding as the most important religious ceremony in her life. In early days there was no such thing as Bat Mitzvah. A boy became a "son" of the commandments, but the girl did not become their "daughter." Bat Mitzvah was introduced only about a generation ago.

Learning and growing

Many peoples have initiation ceremonies when their boys grow up. Only the Jews initiate their boys by letting them prove they can read from the Holy Books, by showing they know something about right and wrong. Bar Mitzvah says a lot about what is important to Jews. So the ceremony takes place in the boy's home —the individual's place—and in the synagogue—the home of the community of Jews.

For the parents of the Bar and Bat Mitzvah, the ceremony is also a great achievement. They have done for their child what their parents did for them. They have fulfilled the commandment in the Shema to "teach them [God's commandments] diligently to your children. . . ." The ceremony will make the parents very happy, for as it has been said: "He who hears his son recite a portion of the Torah is as though he heard it at Mount Sinai."

MORE LEARNING AND GROWING

Confirmation is a kind of "graduation exercise" for religious school. But it is not the end of learning. Even grownups go on studying and growing in wisdom.

The mind never stops growing; it should get more and more understanding. This makes learning so important that it cannot stop. Jews believe that it must continue throughout life. The older you get, the more you need to know. So Bar and Bat Mitzvah do not mark the end of Jewish learning, only the first big step.

Today, a boy or girl of 13 is not like a child of 13 a thousand years ago. Long ago, young girls were often promised in marriage at 13 or soon after. Boys began to earn their living at 13. Today, children stay within the protection of the family for a much longer time.

Besides, a child of 13 today has not studied Judaism nearly as much as children who spent their whole lives on it. So Bar Mitzvah cannot have the same educational meaning today that it had centuries ago.

Confirmation

Because of the great change in Jewish life between the time when the Bar Mitzvah ceremony was being developed and the present, and because Jews are always trying to give their religious ceremonies more present-day meaning, a new religious ceremony began to develop about 150 years ago. It is called *Confirmation*—though that is not a particularly good word for it. The same word describes a Christian ceremony with a different meaning. The Christian young people repeat the promises that were made in their name when they were baptized. For Jews, Confirmation is more than that—it represents religious graduation.

In most cases, it comes about two years after Bar or Bat Mitzvah. But it does not depend on them. In some congregations Confirmation substitutes for Bar or Bat Mitzvah because of the fact that children of 15 or 16 are much better able to understand Judaism than is a child of 12. The ceremony is often held during Shavuot, both because this holiday comes at the end of the school year, and because it is the festival of the giving of the Torah. This makes the celebration doubly joyous. The congregation celebrates both getting the Torah from God and having taught it to the boys and girls who stand before the Ark.

So another moment in a young person's life is shared with his people, and his God. Who he is and what he will be is not a little, lonely, inside thing. A young person—and his future—are important to himself, to his family, to his people, to his God. His time has become part of a bigger, greater time, for it will help bring all men to the End of Days.

5

Marriage

Love and marriage Love is the easiest thing to see—and the hardest to explain. You can see love in the way a mother holds her baby, in the way a father looks at his child. You can see love in the way a scholar holds a great book. And you can see love in the numberless Jews who died rather than deny their God.

The love of a man for a woman, and of a woman for a man, is somewhat the same as all these, and somewhat different. Love between man and woman is the most important thing that can happen to them. And it has the most lasting results. Love, real love, results in marriage, and marriage results in children —and so mankind goes on.

In marriage two people alone become part of each other. Together, they create children and family. Within the family, each person learns to give and to take, to share the good and the bad. Within the family, each person is tied to every other person, yet each person is more truly an individual than if he were alone.

Marriage and God

Jews consider marriage such a miracle that they say it involves not two things, but three. The Talmud puts it this way: A man cannot be fully a man without a wife; a woman cannot be fully a woman without a husband. But together they cannot fulfill themselves without God. God is the third partner.

A Roman lady once asked Rabbi Yosé how long it took God to create the universe.

"Six days," said the Rabbi.

"And what has your God been doing since then?" the lady said.

"Arranging marriages," the Rabbi answered.

"Arranging marriages isn't so hard," the lady said. "I can arrange marriages in a moment." She called for one thousand female slaves and one thousand male slaves to be brought to her, and she lined them up opposite each other, and announced: "You are now married."

LOVE AND MARRIAGE

Real love leads to marriage, and marriage to children. So the family is a center of love and protection.

The next day the slaves appeared before the lady. One had a cracked head, another a cracked lip, a third a broken nose, and so on. "What happened?" the lady cried.

"I don't want him," shouted a slave. "I can't stand her," said a second. "I will not stay with him," cried a third.

The lady went back to the Rabbi and said, "Truly there is no God like your God and making marriages is His most wondrous miracle."

Marriage is so important among Jews that a man is permitted even to sell a Scroll of the Torah to get a wife. It is so important to Jews that the word for marriage is *kiddushin,* meaning "making holy." The love of man and woman is not just feelings or pleasure. It is, at its best, a sharing with God. When a marriage makes a love holy it may look the same on the outside but inside something very deep and important has been added—and the love is changed.

Marriage is so important to Jews not only because of what it does to the family, but for what it means to the Jewish people and their service to God. The new Jewish family will pass on the traditions of past generations. The new parents will give their children a little of what Abraham and Sarah had and what Isaac and Rebecca created. Every marriage means the Jewish people has a future. Every new family means the hope for the Days of the Messiah will not die out but continue until they are real.

Honoring women

Among primitive peoples, a woman was stolen from her parents by force, or she was bought from them like a cow or horse. The woman became the slave and servant of her husband.

Beginning with the earliest chapters of the Bible, women were taken out of the slave-servant class. Since

MAN, WOMAN, AND GOD

Man is fulfilled in woman, and woman in man.
Together, they are fulfilled in God.

then, every body of Jewish law has guarded the rights of the wife. The Ten Commandments say that a child must honor his father *and his mother*. Jewish law says that it is a crime to speak against your father *and your mother*—not just your father.

Jews consider a woman to be different from a man —not less than a man.

The first marriage described in the Bible was that between Isaac and Rebecca. Rebecca wasn't just bought by Isaac. Eliezer chose her for Isaac, not because she was strong and could cook, but because she was kind and tender. The Bible says that Rebecca was asked whether she would accept Isaac as her husband. Rebecca agreed because, the Rabbis say, Isaac was of good character, not because he was rich or important. Those have been the Jewish standards ever since.

Betrothal and engagement

In ancient days there were two separate ceremonies connected with marriage. There was the ceremony of betrothal, the agreement to get married, and there was the actual marriage. These two ceremonies could be a year apart.

Today, we also have two ceremonies: engagement and wedding. But our engagement is not the old betrothal. An engaged couple can simply change their minds and call off the marriage. A betrothed couple were legally bound together although the bride lived in her father's house until the wedding. They could not break up. They would have had to get a divorce.

The custom of betrothal began during the time when a bride was still bought. At the betrothal, the price was agreed upon and a contract was signed. The money was necessary because every member of the family worked, including the young girl. She might tend the flocks, do the washing, weave cloth, help in the kitchen. When she got married, she went to her father-in-law's house and helped there. So, in a way, the father-in-law paid the father for the loss of the daughter's services.

But even in those days, if the bride's father was well-to-do, he gave the bride's price he received to his daughter as a present. Even poor fathers probably gave back part of the money.

To the betrothal ceremony came the entire families of both bride and groom—and it ended with dancing and feasting and merrymaking.

Months later, the groom came to take his bride to his father's house. At that time the bride's price was actually paid—and again there was a great family feast and celebration. But in those days this was the less important ceremony; the more important was the betrothal and contract-signing.

When Jews became farmers and city dwellers instead of shepherds, the betrothal became much less important. It was no longer necessary to give the bride's father a long time to prepare to lose the services of his daughter—and no longer necessary to give him money for her. There were also a lot of poor Jews, and two ceremonies, plus the bride's price, was more than they could afford. So in the first century C.E., the Sanhedrin changed the marriage contract. In the new contract, the groom only promised to pay a certain amount for the bride. He didn't actually have to hand over the money. Instead, the groom gave to his bride a single coin—a *perutah,* the smallest coin at the time—as a token of the bride's price. The rest of the money had to be paid only if the couple got divorced.

The bride's dowry

As it became less important for a father to buy a wife for his son, it became more important for a father to get a husband for his daughter. So fathers offered dowries, money paid by the bride's father to the groom on the marriage. This custom lasted down until modern

THE RIGHTS OF WOMAN

Women have been honored among Jews, and under Jewish law since early Bible times. Children are commanded to honor their mothers and fathers equally. Husband and wife are equal partners in a miracle.

times. In the eighteenth and nineteenth centuries, the bride's father often agreed to provide food and lodging for the couple several years, so the groom could continue his Jewish studies. In more recent times, the bride's father would set up the groom in a business.

But the Talmud warns against letting the dowry influence the choice of bride. "He who takes a wife for the sake of money shall have unworthy children."

The custom of offering a dowry was a burden on poor families, and particularly on orphan girls. So in every Jewish community a special charity fund was set up to provide dowries for poor girls. These dowries were generally not given in cash, but in wedding clothes, kitchen equipment, furniture, and so on. Every girl had some dowry, so money wouldn't stand in the way of her becoming a wife and mother.

Long-ago wedding ceremonies

During the Middle Ages, life was too uncertain for long engagements or betrothals. So both were held on the same day, the betrothal in the morning, the wedding in the afternoon—but still with two ceremonies and two parties. Even this was too much for poor families, so finally the two ceremonies and feasts were combined.

That is the history of the ceremony most Jewish couples have today. In the traditional wedding there still are two parts, one right after the other. If you listen carefully, you can tell when the old betrothal ceremony ends because right afterward they read the marriage contract—the *ketubah*. It is in Aramaic and has a very special sound. Then the marriage ceremony proper, with its blessings, continues.

כְּתוּבָה

The wedding celebration

In one sense, the wedding celebration begins the Sabbath before the marriage day. It is customary then to call the groom to the Bimah during the reading of the Torah to recite the blessings. A special prayer is also recited for him. This is called the *aufruf*, from the Yiddish word meaning "calling up." In some congregations the bride and groom are called up to the Bimah at a Friday evening service and a special prayer for their happiness is said.

At almost all celebrations, people dress up. But there is none to compare to the dressing for a wedding. The bride wears white, a sign of purity. She also wears a veil because Rebecca, in that first wedding in the Bible, "took a veil and covered herself with it." The groom's clothes are left to him and his bride to choose. But they will be quite special.

Wedding customs

Standing with the marriage couple at the ceremony are a best man and a maid or matron of honor. This custom is not new. The Bible story of Samson mentions the groom's best friend standing by him. And the Talmud speaks of the bridal couple having their best friends along with them at the wedding.

Many Jewish wedding customs are very much like the wedding customs of non-Jews. But the one thing that marks a Jewish wedding apart from all others is the *ḥupah,* or canopy, under which the bridal couple stand during the ceremony.

The ḥupah is made of white silk or similar material hung like a small ceiling from four poles. It is often embroidered with a saying from the Bible. A favorite is the one from the Book of Jeremiah which is also used in the blessings: "The voice of mirth and the voice of joy, the voice of the bridegroom and the voice of the bride." Quite often too, the ḥupah is decorated with flowers and green leaves.

The ḥupah reminds us of many things. In Bible days, the bridal couple were led to a specially prepared tent to spend their wedding night. The ḥupah may stand for that tent. It may also stand for the *Tallit* with which a groom used to cover his bride. In ancient days the Tallit was a full cape, not a scarf. When someone took another person under his cape, he was offering his protection. So when a groom put his Tallit around his bride, he took her under his protection. Today, he leads her under the ḥupah to show that he is responsible for her according to God's law.

Ceremony of the ring

The ceremony itself begins with the rabbi reciting the blessing of the betrothal over a cup of wine. He gives the bridegroom a sip from the cup, then the bride. Then the groom places the wedding ring on his bride's finger, and recites the betrothal pledge: "Behold, thou art consecrated unto me by this ring, according to the laws of Moses and Israel."

The ring is the symbol of the bride's price that

WEDDINGS TODAY

Today, in the traditional wedding ceremony, bride and groom stand together, before the Rabbi, under the ḥupah. The betrothal is blessed, the ring is given, the marriage contract is read, then the closing blessings of the marriage ceremony. The wedding feast follows, with music and dancing and the giving of gifts.

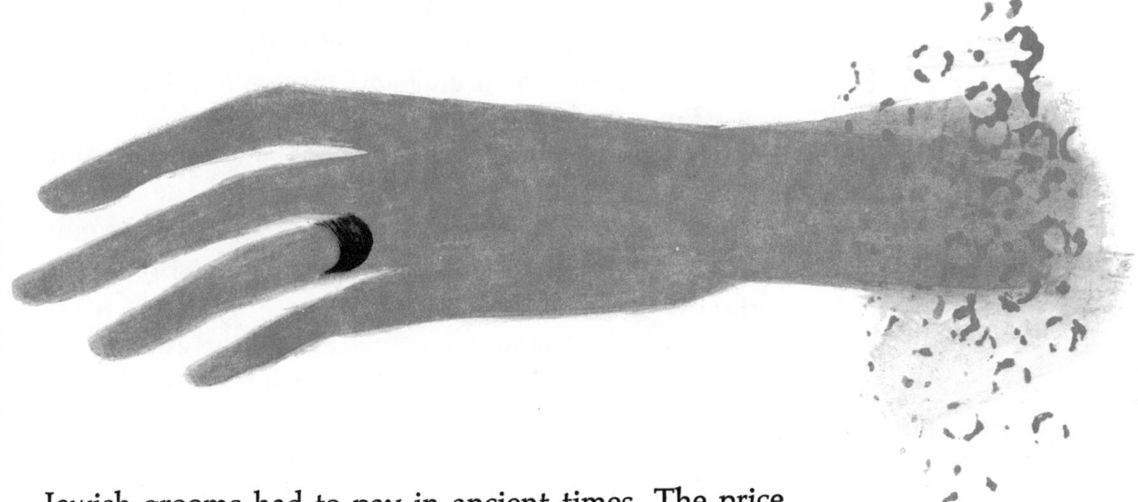

Jewish grooms had to pay in ancient times. The price became the single coin, the perutah, and then a ring. The traditional finger for receiving the wedding ring is the index finger of the *right* hand even though in our society married women wear their rings on the third finger of the left hand.

The marriage contract

After the ceremony of the ring, the rabbi reads the *ketubah,* or marriage contract. The ketubah is written in Aramaic, the everyday language of the Jews two thousand years ago. It gives the date, the place, the names of the bride and groom. It says that the groom asked for the bride's hand and was accepted—the contract cannot be made if the bride does not willingly accept the groom. It lists the amount of money that the groom would have to pay if there is ever a divorce.

Old ketubot were written on parchment and beautifully illustrated. For instance, if the bride's name was Ruth, scenes from the Book of Ruth might decorate the ketubah; if the groom's name was Elijah, there might be pictures from the Elijah story in the Bible. Many are on display today in Jewish museums.

The marriage ceremony and prayer

After the reading of the ketubah, the marriage ceremony proper begins. It opens with the recitation of seven blessings, which end with praise of God "who has created joy and gladness, bridegroom and bride, love and brotherhood, pleasure and delight, peace and harmony."

מזל טוב

Both bride and groom then drink from the same cup of wine. There may be a final prayer or blessing. Then a glass is placed on the floor, and the groom crushes it under his foot. The wedding is over and the guests will probably cry out: *Mazal Tov!* Good luck!

Many reasons are given for the custom of smashing the glass. Some scholars say it has to do with the ancient belief that this will keep evil spirits away. A religious reason is that it reminds us of the destruction of the Temple in Jerusalem. Even on the most joyous occasions we must remember that life includes sorrows. There has been some argument among Jews about breaking the glass since it is only a custom, but for many Jews this custom is as strong as law.

With the ceremony over, the wedding feast begins —with music and dancing and the giving of gifts.

Why June?

Marriages were forbidden by ancient Jewish custom during most of the 50 days between Pesaḥ and Shavuot. It is customary not to celebrate joyous occasions during the three weeks before Tisha be-Av because these are traditionally times of sorrow for our people. So June is the only full month left for weddings between Pesaḥ and the end of summer—for Jews who follow that tradition. (Reform and many Conservative Jews do not.) All Jews agree there should be no weddings on the Sabbath or on holidays.

Against intermarriage

In Bible times, Jews did marry non-Jews—although Abraham had already warned that Isaac must not marry out of the tribe. But in the fifth century B.C.E., Ezra the Scribe banned all marriages between Jews and non-Jews. Ezra's reasons twenty-five centuries ago had to do with protecting the individual and the community of Israel. Those reasons are still given today.

The personal arguments against intermarriage go like this: The chances of happiness are increased if the bride and groom think alike, have the same values, like the same things. Jewish homes, Jewish upbringing, Jewish traditions, even Jewish food, are different from those of non-Jews. These differences lessen the chance of success in a mixed marriage.

The community arguments against intermarriage go like this: For the last two thousand years, Jews have lived dispersed among bigger and stronger peoples, many of whom persecuted the Jews. And for a thousand years before that, Jews lived under foreign emperors and tyrants. Yet the Jews did not die out because they held fast to their own beliefs and customs. If they had intermarried, they would have disappeared.

The family is the big link in the chain that ties the Jewish past to the Jewish future. Without *Jewish* families there will be no more Jews. What you are, and what you stand for, is the addition of what your parents gave you, and what your grandparents gave them, and what your great-grandparents gave your grandparents—and on back. What your children's children will stand for depends on you—and the family you create for them.

6

The home and the family

For many people, their gods live in a special place—in a temple or shrine, or in an idol. But for Jews, God is everywhere. No one place is really more holy to Him than any other. A Ḥasidic Rabbi said: "Where does God live? Wherever man lets Him."

Among most other peoples, a particular kind of person stands between the ordinary man and God—a priest. The priest can do things in the name of God that cannot be done by others.

Among Jews, every man is equal before God. The rabbi has no special authority. The government may give him special rights, but he has no extra authority from God.

Every place in which a Jew is, is also God's special place. And that is true of the place in which man spends most of his time, his home. That is where his children learn, where the Seder is held, the sukkah is

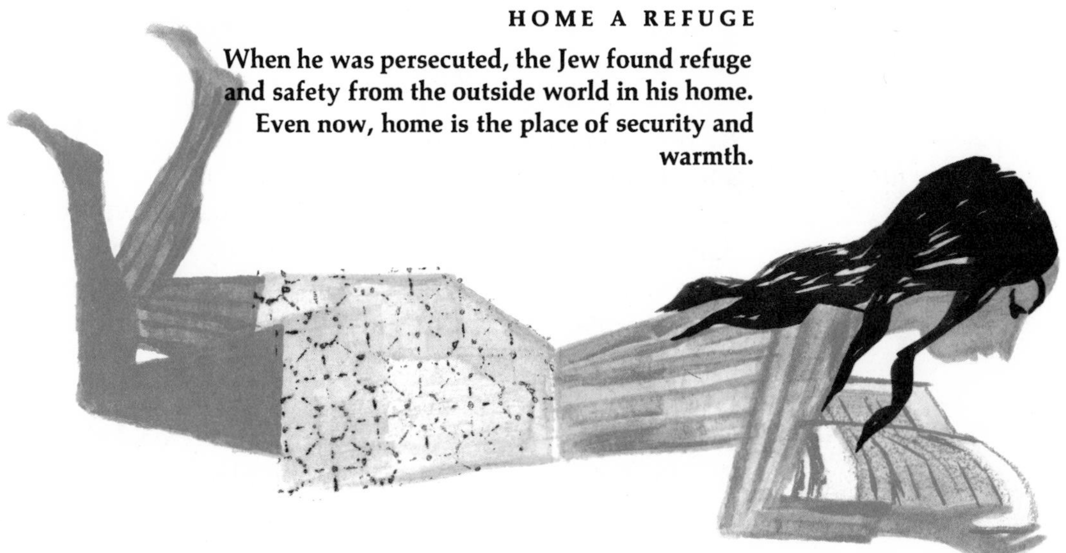

HOME A REFUGE

When he was persecuted, the Jew found refuge and safety from the outside world in his home. Even now, home is the place of security and warmth.

built, and the Ḥanukkah lights are lit. For a Jew, his home is a small temple to God.

A woman's duties

And in the home, woman is most important.

Traditionally a man is required to fulfill all the 613 commandments; a woman to do only those that will not interfere with her duties as a wife and mother.

In the traditional synagogue, men are most important. But in the home, that small temple, woman sets the tone; woman gives the flavor; woman decides whether it will be truly Jewish or not.

Our Rabbis said, "Whatever blessing dwells in the home comes from the wife."

In Bible days, a home included many more people than we now think of as making up a family. Married children and the old folks all lived together with the family. So a household might have 40 or 50 people in it. There were no synagogues then. A few members of the family went to Jerusalem on the three pilgrim festivals—Pesaḥ, Shavuot, Sukkot—but most religious ceremonies took place in the home. The home was the center of religion, as it was of life.

Home as the center

As the Jews began to live away from the Land of Israel, and among non-Jews, the home became even more important. In the days of the ghettos, it was often dangerous to go outside the ghetto by day and Jews were not allowed out after dark. Then the home was the only place in which most Jews could find warmth and safety.

Our families are much smaller now. We are not afraid to go out of our homes into the world outside. But for Jews the home remains the place where we are most often in touch with Judaism. We spend a good part of our lives in places that have no particular Jewish feeling. Schools, offices, work places, are the same for Jews and non-Jews. The synagogue is a Jewish place. But few people spend more than a few hours a week there. We get our sense of being Jewish, our understanding of what Judaism teaches us to be, mostly from the home.

THE HOME A LITTLE TEMPLE

The home of a Jew is a special place. It is the place where Jewish customs and ways are lived and Jewish children learn about God.

But what makes a home Jewish?

Jewish and non-Jewish homes look alike. They have the same lawns and shrubs in the suburbs; the same apartments in the city. They have the same furniture, the same television sets, the same appliances, the same drapes.

There are differences in small things—and larger differences in feeling.

The Mezuzah

מְזוּזָה

The first difference you see on entering many Jewish homes is on the doorpost—the *Mezuzah*. Today, many people put the Mezuzah only on their front doorpost. Traditionally, the Mezuzah was nailed on every doorpost leading into every room in the house (except the bathroom).

The Mezuzah is a small box with a piece of parchment inside. On it are written the first two paragraphs of the Shema—to the commandment, "thou shalt write them [the Laws] upon the doorposts of thy house and upon thy gates." On the other side of the piece of parchment is written the single word, *Shaddai*, "the Almighty." The parchment is rolled with the Shema on the inside and the word *Shaddai* on the outside. If there is a window in the Mezuzah, you can see *Shaddai* in it. Some modern Mezuzot are made so that you can see all the Bible verses.

The Mezuzah is nailed—not hung—on the upper part of the doorpost to the right as you enter the house. It

MARKS OF A JEWISH HOME

A Jewish home may be known by outward signs such as the Mezuzah. But more important in making a home Jewish are Jewish ways of thinking, and feeling, and acting toward others.

leans a little, the upper part leaning toward the house, the lower part to the world outside.

On entering and leaving the house, an observant Jew touches the Mezuzah with his fingers and then kisses the fingers.

The Mezuzah is a symbol, a sign, that this is a house whose people believe in the One God and follow His Law. In that house, there should be peace. There should be no quarreling, no viciousness, and no injustice. From that house goes forth charity and righteousness, for every Jew leaving it is reminded of his duties as he goes into the world.

For many centuries the Mezuzah had another, more practical purpose. Jews entering a strange town could find a place to stay by looking for the house with the Mezuzah. And Jews escaping from mobs could find help by looking for the house with the Mezuzah.

Keeping Kashrut

כַּשְׁרוּת

Traditionally, the most obvious difference between a Jewish home and Christian home was in *Kashrut*. In a Jewish home the dietary laws were observed.

There has been a great deal of argument during the last hundred years about these food laws. Some Jews say that there is no longer any need for strict observance of Kashrut; others say that Kashrut is necessary to the continuance of Jewish life.

Jewish attitude toward food

But whatever side one may take on this question, there is no argument about the Jewish attitude toward food. An animal eats food; a civilized man (and Jews always considered themselves civilized) eats a meal—there's a big difference between them. That's why Jews frowned on eating in the street. To do so, says the Talmud, is to act like an animal. A Jew, the Rabbis said, should always act as if his table were the altar in the Temple and his food was a sacrifice to God.

Food is a particular gift from God. So Jews eat with pleasure but with a certain dignity. Before each new food we are expected to say a blessing. The blessing is a way of saying thanks. It ties us to our God whenever we eat. Every day, at every meal, our time is linked to this.

There are blessings for all manner of food, and all these blessings are almost alike except for the last few words.

בָּרוּךְ אַתָּה יְיָ. אֱלֹהֵינוּ מֶלֶךְ הָעוֹלָם. הַמּוֹצִיא (בּוֹרֵא) . . .

Blessed art Thou, Lord our God, . . . who brings forth (or creates) . . .

There's a blessing for bread (bread from the earth); there is a blessing for fruit (fruit of the tree); there is a blessing for vegetables (fruit of the earth); there is a blessing for grains other than bread (various kinds of food); there is a blessing for meat, fish, eggs, and so on (by whose word all things exist); and there is a blessing for wine (fruit of the vine).

That's why a Jew is required to wash his hands before sitting down to a meal. Cleanliness is important, but the washing before the meal also reminds us that the priest had to be clean inside and outside before performing the sacrifice. In a way, we are now the priests, serving God every day.

Origin of Kashrut

With so much importance placed on food, it is easy to understand why Judaism cares so much about what is eaten and how it is prepared. Some people say the laws of Kashrut were originally laws of cleanliness and health. They say that pigs eat garbage and can give man a very bad disease called *trichinosis*, caused by a kind of tiny worm. So Jews were forbidden to eat pigs. There are also sanitary and health reasons for not eating oysters and clams and shrimp.

These health reasons were not the real reason for Kashrut. The Torah does not give us any special reasons. It just gives us the laws. Modern scholars have suggested that this is the way the laws began: In ancient days the Jews' idol-worshiping neighbors ate pig and boiled young goats in the milk of the mother goat. The laws of Kashrut forbade those acts and so separated the Jews from the idol-worshipers. That is an interesting idea. But most Jews obeyed the dietary laws—and many still do—simply because the laws are based on commandments in the Torah and following them is a mark of respect and obedience to God.

Today, many Jews continue to obey the laws of Kashrut because they are a particular mark of the Jew. Many Jews obey these laws out of loyalty and respect for the traditions of their fathers. Some Jews keep some dietary laws and do not keep others. Some Jews obey the laws at home but not outside the home. And some Jews do not obey the dietary laws at all.

The question is not an easy one to decide if you care about being Jewish. It is one you should think about carefully now and as you get older. Your teachers and rabbi can help you understand what is involved and your parents will share their experience with you.

One thing, however, must be said. Every Jew, regardless of his own feelings about Kashrut, should be respectful of the feelings and beliefs of others. If his parents keep kosher, he keeps kosher so long as he is in their home. If he visits people who follow the laws of Kashrut, he respects his hosts' beliefs. If his synagogue requires certain rules of eating and conduct, he follows them when in or near the synagogue.

Jewish hospitality

Hospitality is another mark of the Jewish home. Of course, many people are just as hospitable as Jews. But for the Jews hospitality to the stranger is a religious commandment. One of the earliest stories in the Bible is of Abraham's hospitality to Lot, and of his hospitality to the three men who turned out to be angels.

In the Middle Ages, travel was dangerous and uncomfortable for everyone. For the Jewish traveler, the dangers were much greater. But every Jewish traveler knew that he would find a place to stay and food to eat in a strange town—if not by going to the synagogue then by looking for a house with a Mezuzah.

A popular Yiddish writer, Mordecai Spector, tells of the time the beggars of one shtetl in Eastern Europe went on strike. They were all invited to attend the wedding of the daughter of the town's richest man. And they all refused to go unless they were given a ruble each. As a result the wedding could not be held

JEWISH HOSPITALITY

Hospitality to strangers is a commandment of Jewish law. Not only friends and family, but strangers, the poor, the homeless are to be welcomed to our feasts and offered the shelter of our home.

—because in those days a proper Jewish wedding had to be blessed by the presence of the poor at the feast. What could the father of the bride do? He finally gave in, and everyone had a wonderful time.

And to this day, we open the Pesaḥ Seder with the invitation: "Let all who are hungry come and share this Seder with us."

Religious objects and symbols

At one time, almost every Jewish home had a mizraḥ plaque on the east wall of the living room. *Mizraḥ* means "east," and the mizraḥ showed the direction of Jerusalem, where Jews faced in prayer. Today, a Jewish home will often have pictures, etchings, or paintings which show Jewish scenes or symbols.

There are other beautiful Jewish objects to be seen, the ones used for the Jewish holidays. There will be a Ḥanukkah menorah, a pair of Sabbath candleholders, a Seder plate, a Kiddush cup, perhaps a spice box for Havdalah.

But things alone do not make a home Jewish. People do. The way the people in the house live, and the way they live together.

There is a way of looking at things and laughing at things that is particularly Jewish—just as there is a style that is particularly Irish or Italian or Black or Mexican.

In a Jewish house it seems that there is always a sense of preparing. The house is very calendar conscious, very time conscious. Every few days, it seems, the house is preparing for Shabbat. And every few weeks for another holiday—for the Seder, for Sukkot, for Ḥanukkah, for Purim, and on and on. There are Bar Mitzvah and Bat Mitzvah celebrations to prepare for, and weddings and Berit Milah—yes, and funeral meals, too. There are gifts to be bought; New Year cards to send; special services to remember.

WOMAN'S ROLE

The home is the special responsibility of the woman. She arranges its ceremonies and celebrations. She sets its tone and feeling. She is so important in making the home a place of warmth and security for her family that traditional law says a woman is excused from the commandments that might interfere with her duties as a wife and mother.

The mother's role

So the house is in a constant state of preparing—and the most important person in the house for this preparing is the mother. For example, the most important religious event that takes place in the home is the celebration of the Sabbath. And the mother begins this celebration with the lighting of the candles and the recitation of the blessing.

At every festival too, she will begin the rituals by lighting her candles. The family mood at the festive meals will largely be set by her.

Once, says a story in the Talmud, there was a very good and pious couple. But although they had been married for many years, they did not have any children. So they were divorced and each married again. The man married a bad woman—and soon turned bad himself. The woman married an evil man—and soon the evil man became good. So, said the Rabbis, whether a man is good or bad depends on his wife. A bad woman can turn a good man bad; a good woman can turn a bad man good.

In praise of women

For all these reasons, and for his own personal ones, the husband recites a hymn in praise of his wife—and of women—every Friday evening:

A woman of valor who can find?
For her price is far above rubies.
Her husband's heart can trust her safely,
And he has no lack of gain.
She brings him good and not evil
All the days of her life.
She looks for wool and flax
And willingly works them with her hands.
She is like the merchant ship;
She brings food from afar.
She gets up while it is yet night,
And prepares food for her household and a portion for her servants . . .
She stretches out her hand to the poor;
Yes, she reaches forth her hands to the needy.
Strength and dignity are her clothing;
And she looks confidently to the future.
She opens her mouth with wisdom;
And the law of kindness is on her tongue.
She looks well to the ways of her household,
And is never idle.
Her children rise up and call her blessed;
Her husband also, and he praises her;
"Many daughters have done valiantly.
But you excel them all."
Grace can be false, and beauty can be vain;
But a woman that reveres the Lord, is always worthy of praise.
Give her of the fruit of her hands;
And let her works praise her in the gates.

(Proverbs 31:10-31)

Valuing Jewish ways

What makes a home truly Jewish, tying together the love and understanding and fairness, is the belief in Judaism and its practice. Sometimes it is heard out loud in Bible verses, in blessings, or in prayers. Sometimes it is seen in ceremonial acts or objects. Mostly it is felt deep inside oneself, as naturally as one feels at home there. For when the family cares about being Jewish they create a Jewish home and family.

7
Death

Death and life

Death and life are two parts of the same process. If life is to continue, there must be death. The flower must die so that the seed can be freed. A tree dies, is enfolded into the ground, enriching the soil for new plants.

Death is natural; it comes to all things that have the spark of life. Only those things that never lived will never die.

We should not welcome death—but neither should we fear it. Our Rabbis taught:

"This is like two ships in the harbor. People ignore the one arriving and celebrate the one going away. The ship that is leaving the harbor must still face rough seas and storms and great danger. We should rather rejoice over the ship returning from its voyage because it is safely back from the perils of the sea."

When a person is born, no one knows whether he will be good or bad, whether he will have an easy life or a miserable one. So why rejoice? When a person leaves this world in peace and with a good name, we can rejoice because his struggle is over and successful.

Comfort in time of death

Still, it is very hard to lose something or someone we love. We feel hurt when a person dies; we feel that someone dear to us has been taken away. We do not understand why he has gone. We ourselves feel lost.

During these times of loss and grief, we cannot think clearly for ourselves. To take care of such times people have developed rites for death. These rites not only tell us what to do, they help us understand death as best men can understand it. They keep us from being lonely and lost for they remind us that death has come to others before—and will come to many after us. They make our loss bearable.

This is different from all the other special days in a life. It is not a celebration, but a time of sadness, of being solemn. But again there are family and friends to be with, Jewish things to do and think about, a God to be with in difficult as in beautiful times.

The Jewish ceremonies around death express our love for the person who died. These rituals teach us that love continues after death. They teach us the importance of life. And they give our friends and relatives an opportunity to express their love for us.

In the old days, when Jews lived in small towns and villages, everyone was expected to stop his work and join in the funeral of a dead neighbor. Even study of the Torah was to be interrupted by a funeral. As life grew more complicated it became impossible for everyone to stop work at every funeral. So a beautiful custom developed: When a funeral passed you on the street, you turned and walked with the funeral, if only for a few steps, to show that your heart went with the family of the dead person. Today cities are so big and

TIME AND DEATH

Time brings both birth and death to all living things. Both are part of the same life process.

funerals so frequent we don't even do that. But we do still show our respect one way. Drivers never cut through a line of cars in a funeral. Even if the traffic light has turned we give them the right of way.

Life after death

Many scholars believe that the ancient Hebrews did not believe in life after death.

The Rabbis of the Talmud asked why the Bible, in recording the death of King David, says: "And David slept with his fathers"? Why, they asked, does not the Bible say, "And David died"?

Because, answered the Sages, David left a son (Solomon) who walked in the good ways of his father, and who continued David's noble deeds. Therefore, David was really not dead. He lived on through the good deeds of his son.

That was the most important way in which the Hebrews of Bible times saw men living after death.

By the time of one of the last Biblical books, Daniel, the Jews came to believe that there was something beyond death. Not a physical life but some continuation of the spirit of individual man. The spirit that is in us continues in some way after our bodies have died, in a way known only to God. They also believed that after the Messiah came God would do away with death once and for all. Following a picture given in Ezekiel, Chapter 37, the famous vision of the dry bones, they

Although death is inevitable, the loss of a loved one is painful. The rites and ceremonies of death help bear the loss. Friends and relatives gather to help the family feel less lonely. They help by doing the work of the house, they help by giving an extra measure of love.

believed God would give life back to the dead. He would put the spirits into the bodies, now made new and whole. Then the real life after death would start. The way in which we treat our dead, and the way in which we mourn our dead—the religious ceremonies of death—are still expressions of these beliefs.

Rituals and customs

The new customs of death and burial developed slowly over the years that followed. These are the major customs of death followed by our grandfathers, and us:

שְׁמַע

A Jew is supposed to die as he lived, proclaiming God. With his last breath a Jew tries to pronounce the Shema: "Hear, O Israel, the Lord our God, the Lord is One." He is God for us in death as in life.

From the moment of death until the burial, the body is not supposed to be left alone. This duty would be too hard for a member of the family of the dead person, so in ancient days it was usually done by friends and neighbors. In time, this mitzvah was taken over by a community group called the *Ḥevrah Kaddisha*—the Holy Brotherhood—who not only watched the dead person through the night but also prepared the body for burial. (It was washed and dressed in a simple linen garment.) Such Ḥevrot existed in all Jewish communities because there was no such thing as undertakers. Membership in the Ḥevrah was a great honor because only the most pious and respected Jews were admitted. All this showed respect for the dead person's body. It was to go to its last resting place in dignity.

Burial

The Romans generally burned their dead. The Persians left their dead on high towers to be eaten by birds. The Jews laid their dead to rest in the earth—and because this was so different from the customs of others around them, burial became specially important.

In Biblical times and for centuries after, a Jew was

buried the same day he died. This became a hardship in large communities where more time was needed to arrange the funeral and notify friends and relatives. So the time was extended twenty-four hours. Today, a Jew is usually buried the day after he dies. But never on the Sabbath or the first day of a holiday. If time is needed to let the relatives gather they may wait even another day.

The very short time between death and burial may have had a health reason in ancient times. But there was also a sound religious reason: Jews do not believe in mourning too long or too hard. Life is more important than death. Extreme mourning seems to make death more important than living. Burying the dead soon after death occurs limits the time of greatest grief and pain. And one can start living one's life again a little sooner.

The body of a dead person is washed and dressed in burial clothes. In ancient times people thought they could show the depth of their grief by dressing the dead in the richest clothes possible. Often a poor family spent money needed for living to pay for a funeral. About two thousand years ago, Rabban Gamaliel, the head of the Sanhedrin, the chief Jewish court, ordered that when he died he was to be dressed in simple white robes. His pupils asked that they too be buried in simple clothes. Since that time, many Jews have followed this custom.

In ancient times, too, the dead were often laid in their graves without coffins. Later, health laws required coffins and these became customary. The traditional Jewish coffin is a simple wooden box, put together without nails or metal ornaments or fancy carvings.

Wherever possible, some Jews place a bag of earth from the Holy Land in the coffin under the head of the deceased, as a substitute for burial there.

In the days of the Rabbis it was the custom for a scholar to give a speech, called a eulogy, after the prayers at the funeral of a wise man or important leader. Soon, if there was no speech, people would say: "He couldn't have been much." So the custom arose of giving eulogies at funerals, as we do today.

The funeral service

The main service today takes place in a funeral home, or if the person had distinguished himself, in the synagogue. It is not a long service. There are generally a few psalms and prayers. The rabbi may choose whichever he wishes. Some are used very often. Not everyone will go on to the cemetery, which is often quite a distance away. There the ceremony is very much shorter, with no speeches.

At the cemetery, the coffin is lowered into the ground. At a traditional funeral, each mourner throws three shovelfuls of earth into the grave. The outer garment of each member of the family of the dead person is cut. (Today, the cut is frequently made in a piece of cloth pinned to the mourner's clothes.) This custom is very old and comes down to us from the Bible custom of tearing the clothes to show grief.

THE END OF DAYS

So long as time goes on, death continues. But Jews believe that the spirit of a man lives on after his body has died. Death will end only with the coming of the Kingdom of God.

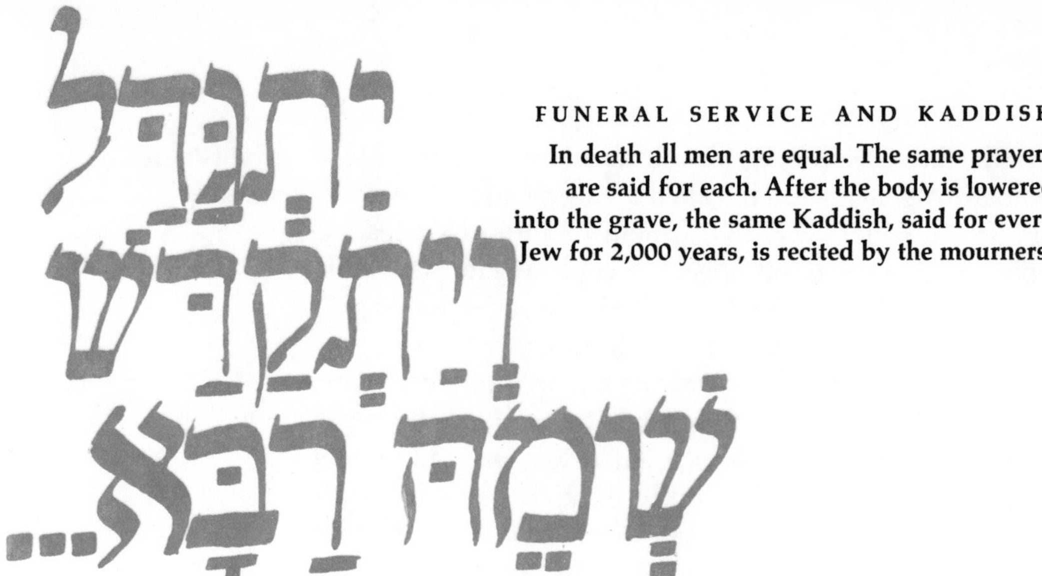

FUNERAL SERVICE AND KADDISH

In death all men are equal. The same prayers are said for each. After the body is lowered into the grave, the same Kaddish, said for every Jew for 2,000 years, is recited by the mourners.

The Kaddish

קדיש

After the coffin has been lowered into the grave, the chief mourners recite the *Kaddish*.

The Kaddish does not speak of death. It is a prayer that God will bring His Kingdom and His peace soon. In the days of the Rabbis the Kaddish was recited after every lecture on the Torah. From this arose the custom of reciting the Kaddish after the eulogy. So the Kaddish came to be recited at the funeral of all Jews—and is today. Of course if the Kingdom of God did come, death would be ended. Life after death would be real for all. That is the thought that makes the Kaddish prayer mean so much at the time of death.

Respect for the dead

Because the cemetery is the place where a person's body is put, Jews treat it with great respect. The body is, of course, dead, and only the spirit lives on. Still, that is what remains of each person and so we treat graves with something of the honor we gave the dead when they were alive.

We show our respect for the dead and we comfort the living by a number of customs in mourning. Mourning is a kind of turning away from life. And life is always more important than death. So rules were made by Jews to limit the kinds of mourning and the length of mourning.

After the funeral, there are three stages of Jewish mourning: seven days of complete mourning; 30 days of deep mourning for members of the immediate family; and 11 months of lesser mourning.

Kindness to the living

In the hours immediately after death there is no mourning. One must arrange for the funeral, notify relatives and friends, take care of one's affairs. The official mourning does not begin until after the funeral. And even then not until after the mourners have returned home and have eaten the funeral meal. This rule was made because the family of the dead person are too overcome with grief to think of eating. Making the funeral meal part of the rites forces them to eat.

The funeral meal is prepared and served by relatives and friends. This is another thoughtful mitzvah. It gives one's neighbors an opportunity to express their friendship for the mourners. It shows the mourners that they have loving friends.

Here too, as in burial clothes and coffins, the Talmud requires equality. The Rabbis said—

> *Formerly those who came to a wealthy mourner with the first meal after a funeral would bring food in golden baskets. To poor mourners, however, food was brought in wicker baskets. The poor felt humiliated. So the Rabbis ordered that food be brought to all mourners in wicker baskets.*
>
> *To wealthy mourners, they brought wine in flasks of white glass; to the poor in flasks of colored glass. Again the poor felt humiliated because white glass was more costly. Therefore it was ordered that wine should be brought to all in colored flasks.*
>
> *Formerly, the wealthy were buried in fancy caskets, the poor in cheap coffins. This, too, was changed and now all who die, rich or poor, are buried in inexpensive caskets.*

Sitting Shivah

The first seven days after the funeral is the period called *Shivah* (from the Hebrew word for "seven").

During the Shivah period the family of the dead person stay at home and are cared for by relatives, friends, and neighbors. Traditionally, the mourners do not wear leather shoes; they sit low, on stools or boxes instead of chairs. Services are conducted in the home every day, except on the Sabbath when the mourners may leave the house to go to the synagogue. A minyan is required for these daily services and it is a special mitzvah to be part of this minyan. Few Jews would refuse such a request.

Limits to mourning

In the 30-day period most of one's normal activities can continue. Still, specially joyous things like getting married or buying new clothes are avoided. This is a compromise between two opposite feelings. The mourning period would be very long if left to the mourners. On the other hand, if the soul of the dead person is with God, mourning shouldn't be so necessary. So a compromise was made. One should show one's deep grief for the 7 days, medium grief for the 30 days, and some grief for almost a year. So for a period of 11 months the Kaddish is said every day by the immediate relatives of the dead person.

Usually within the period of mourning, a stone is placed on the grave as a monument. Such a stone, a *matzevah,* is by now a custom as strong as law. The matzevah, too, should not be so elaborate that it would shame those families who cannot afford a fancy stone.

Remembering loved ones

A grave is not a shrine or a holy place. The cemetery is, however, a place of remembrance. So Jews visit graves during the month before Rosh Hashanah, the holiday of remembrance, sometimes on the anniversary of the death, or whenever they wish.

Each year, on the anniversary of the death, the relatives stand with the mourners in the synagogue and say the Kaddish. In many synagogues it is customary on the Sabbath to read the names of persons whose *yahrzeit*—death anniversary—is being remembered that week. Often the family will make a special donation to charity. It is also a custom to remember the yahrzeit by lighting a special candle that burns for twenty-four hours.

In the Middle Ages, following the massacre of thousands of Jews during the Crusades, a special memorial prayer for these martyrs was added to the Jewish prayer book. This prayer is called *Yizkor*, from the opening words of the prayer—"May God remember." In time, this Yizkor prayer became general, covering all Jews who had died. Sephardic Jews recite it only on Yom Kippur.

Most American synagogues say the Yizkor prayer also as part of the services bringing Pesaḥ, Shavuot, and Sukkot to an end.

Most of what has been said here is about someone in whose family a death has taken place. But death brings duties to all Jews who hear about it. Our Jewish people stand close together when things are sad. We help and encourage each other. We give people strength to get by the bad times. We stand by them until they can take up life again.

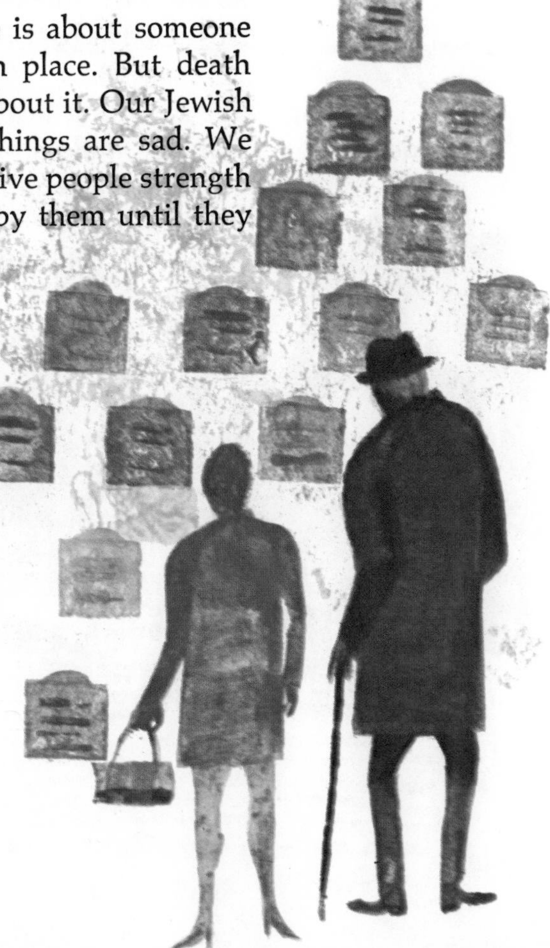

LOVE AND REMEMBRANCE

Remembrance of the dead is shown by visits to the cemetery, by saying the Kaddish on each anniversary of the death, by the Yizkor prayer, and sometimes by a gift to charity in the name of the loved one.

Man's life span

Death is sad, but also necessary. It is a part of everyone's time. So it must be accepted—even when it comes to those we love and to those who, we believe, are not yet ready for death. Jews have always questioned why some good people die young. They did not live the 70 years the Bible says is a full lifetime. There is no good answer to this question. We can only trust God.

We do not understand what force holds an atom together. We do not understand how a salmon, roaming the seas for years, returns to the exact spot where she was born to lay her eggs. We do not understand how a tiny thing called a *chromosome*, too small to be seen with the eye, controls the color of our eyes and the size to which we will grow. We do not understand many of the wonders of life and the universe. Neither do we fully understand death, but still we accept it and trust God as best we can.

Accepting death

But accepting death is not the same as welcoming it:

In the middle of the last century, a plague ravaged the city of Kovno in Lithuania all through the summer. Thousands died, and those who did not die were sick and weak. The Days of Awe came, and still the plague did not let up. On Yom Kippur, the great Rabbi of Kovno, Israel Lipkin, stood before his congregation and

saw that they were flushed with fever and trembling with weakness. And he announced, "For the good of the people and of Israel, there shall be no fasting this Yom Kippur."

There was an outcry from among the congregation. Some said they would die as they had lived, following the commandments. Others said the plague was only another trial sent by God, and they would accept it.

But standing before the Ark, on Yom Kippur, Rabbi Israel Lipkin drew forth a piece of bread and, after reciting the blessing *ha-Motzi,* ate it. There was a gasp from the congregation, and the Rabbi answered it:

"It is commanded that you shall live to serve your God. If you fast, you will die. If you break the commandment to fast on Yom Kippur, you will live. God calls you to life."

Choosing life

So we chose life. But we also accept death as a part of life, of everyone's life. By meeting it as part of our people and by accepting it as part of God's order for the world, we make death another part of our life plan. Everything in our time, from birth to death, helps us to be true to ourselves and build a better world. We may only be one person in a great world but this way we know that with our people we will use our time to bring the Days of the Messiah.

Your own time is your life.
There is another time that you share with everyone.
It is the time set by sun and moon,
The days and weeks, the months and years,
The seasons of spring, summer, autumn, winter.
This time belongs to everyone,
And it goes on forever.
One season follows another until the first comes around again,
And year follows year.
Sooner or later, the events that measure time repeat themselves.

But not the events of history.
There was only one Exodus,

Time and the community

One giving of the Torah,
One journey through the wilderness to the Holy Land.
Our people celebrated everyone's time
Because they were part of everyone.
But they also celebrated their own time,
When great things happened to them.
They put the two together—
Everyone's time and their own time.
What happened in nature
And what happened to the Jews.
They made a special Jewish time,
A special Jewish calendar.
This calendar links you with your people,
In the journey to the Days of the Messiah.

THE WEEKS

Life and history sound very important.
But they are both made up of days and weeks.
Day by day, week by week,
We spend our lives doing good, or bad, in history.

If we waste our days,
If we throw them away,
If we do not care how we spend our weeks,
Our lives will be empty and our world full of fear.

But if we learn to see each day as an opportunity,
And use each week to move ahead,
If we learn to fill our days with good deeds and love for others,
If we look upon our days and weeks as our people did—
As a chance to serve God,
As an opportunity to help Him build the Kingdom of God on earth,
Then our time will have been important—
To ourselves, to our people, to the world, to God.

8

The Sabbath

A day of joy

Most holidays come once each year, repeating year after year. But the most important holiday for Jews (except for Yom Kippur) comes each week: the Shabbat.

What can be so important about a holiday that repeats 52 times a year?

The Shabbat marks the difference between man and all other creatures that live in the universe; the Shabbat celebrates the tie between God and the Jews.

Man is different from everything else in nature. He is different from the animals of land and sea; different from the trees and grasses that grow in earth; different from the seas and mountains that cover the earth.

To stop for a while

Nothing interferes with the regular rhythm of nature—except man. The sun rises and sets each day, without stop. The moon comes up, grows, gets small, and disappears every 29 days, without stop. The tides fill and

Dispersed among a hundred nations, the Sabbath has bound the Jews together through the centuries. And it has bound the Jewish people to God. It gave them rest and cheer and strength. It helped them to remember who they were—and their mission on earth.

the tides ebb without stop. The grass comes up every spring; the trees bear fruit every fall, without halt. Only death stops the regular rhythm of natural things—but death, too, is part of the unending circle of life.

But man can and does stop his work, stop his running, stop following his animal instincts. He stops even though his work isn't finished, even though there is more he wants to do. He rests, he thinks. He looks back on what he has won, which other creatures do not do. He looks ahead, as animals and trees cannot; he chooses the way he will go. He thanks God for all His help and asks God for continuing help in choosing wisely.

He does this on the Shabbat. The Shabbat is the greatest of holidays because then man becomes truly a man, different from all the animals.

The Shabbat also reminds Jews of the promises their forefathers made with God.

Circumcision is the chief mark of that covenant, but a Jew is circumcised only once in his lifetime. The Shabbat gives every Jew a chance to renew this agreement with God—every seven days. No one can keep the Shabbat for another; every person has to keep his own Shabbat in his own way. And every time a Jew keeps the Shabbat, he shows that he personally accepts the covenant all Jews entered into some four thousand years ago. He accepts God all over again and knows God accepts him and all His people to serve Him.

Keeping the Sabbath

Six holidays are mentioned in the Torah: Pesaḥ, Shavuot, Sukkot, Rosh Hashanah, Yom Kippur—and the Shabbat. Only one of these is mentioned—commanded—in the Ten Commandments: the Shabbat.

The Ten Commandments are written twice in the Torah, once in the Book of Exodus and once in the Book of Deuteronomy. Each gives another reason for celebrating the Shabbat.

In Exodus we are told to remember the Shabbat because "in six days the Lord made heaven and earth, the sea, and all that is in them, and He rested on the seventh day. That is why the Lord blessed the Sabbath day and made it holy." The Sabbath comes to remind us of God's work in creation. And part of what He created was rest and holiness. In this, and in all other things, we should follow God's example.

In Deuteronomy we are told to observe the Shabbat because "you were a slave in the land of Egypt, and the Lord your God brought you out of there . . . therefore the Lord your God commanded you to keep the Sabbath day." The Sabbath comes to remind us of God's gift of freedom. Each week we remember that we were slaves who worked without rest and celebrate the gift of freedom.

So for century after century, the Shabbat was the

TAKING STOCK OF OURSELVES

Sabbath gives a person a chance to stand aside from his work and his everyday concerns. He can consider what he has been doing—and what he and other Jews can do to help bring the time of peace and justice—the Days of the Messiah.

glue that kept the Jews together. During the years when the Jews lived in places where they were oppressed and the days were poisoned by fear, the Shabbat was the breath of fresh air once a week that kept them alive. It gave them hope, courage, strength, and a feeling that they were not alone in history. The great Jewish writer Aḥad Ha-Am said, "More than Israel [the Jews] kept the Sabbath, the Sabbath kept Israel."

Origins of Shabbat

How did the Jews get the Shabbat and how did it change and grow over the centuries?

In ancient times most people divided the month into three parts instead of four. The ancient Egyptians, the Greeks, Romans, Chinese, the people of India, used a ten-day week instead of a seven-day week. This ten-day week is still used in Viet Nam, Laos, Cambodia.

The word *Shabbat* probably comes to us from the ancient Babylonians. They had a day, the day of the full moon, called *Shabbatum*. On Shabbatum, Babylonians stayed home because they believed the streets were filled with goblins and devils and other evil spirits. Even the king was not permitted to leave the palace on that day. The Hebrews, who lived in Babylon before they came to Canaan, probably brought this word with them but they changed the idea entirely. From a day of fear they made a day of gladness; from a day of terror they made a day of joy.

Shabbat in home and synagogue

When the First Temple stood in Jerusalem, it was the center of the rituals that are so important in religion. But for most people, going to the Temple meant a long journey. Even those who lived in Jerusalem went to the Temple mainly on the three great pilgrimage holidays. For most Jews the Shabbat was celebrated at home as a day of complete rest from work and from everyday cares.

Over the centuries of the Kingdom of Judah, the people grew lax about keeping the Shabbat. The prophet Jeremiah warned them, "hallow ye the Sabbath day." Then came war and the destruction of the First Temple. Many Jews were taken to Babylon as captives.

In Babylon there was no Temple, and so no central place to celebrate the religion of the Jews. If Judaism was to continue, the people had to see to it themselves; their religion was no longer the responsibility of the priests. So the Shabbat became more important. It could be celebrated almost anywhere, in small gatherings and, especially, in the home. That's probably when the synagogue got started. It could be any place. So every Jew could regularly take part in observance of the Shabbat, which probably meant to hear stories of the forefathers or words of the prophets. Later it meant reading the holy books and then saying prayers.

When the Jews returned to Palestine under Ezra and Nehemiah they brought with them the synagogue and the new importance of the Shabbat. Even when the Second Temple was built and the priests began sacrifices again, synagogues continued and spread throughout the countryside. And the Shabbat remained not only the main synagogue holiday, but the main home holiday.

A different kind of day

Then, 2,300 years ago, Alexander the Great, the Greek king, conquered most of the world, including the Land of Israel. The Jews became part of the Greek world.

Most Jews knew that the Greek customs were tied to Greek religion, to the worship of idols, so they kept the Shabbat. Their teachers told them:

"A master says to his workmen, work for me six days and take one day for yourself. God says, work for yourself six days, and give Me only one day."

However, there were some Jews who wanted to follow the free and easy ways of the Greeks. So, because it was one of the most easily seen differences between the Jews and the Gentiles, celebrating the Shabbat became a most important religious act.

On Shabbat there is no difference in the sky, no difference in the season. The difference is in the Jewish people. They count days—and when they get to seven they make it a holiday. It is the holiday when, for Jews, all the world changes, when gloom changes to gladness as the candles are lit, when the best food is eaten and the best clothes worn. The Talmud says the Shabbat is like a queen because when she appears even the most miserable hut becomes a palace.

Shabbat is different, too, because on that day there is a feeling that all the usual differences between men disappear. That day, it seems there are no rich and poor, no powerful and weak. In his own home each man is a prince, a high priest. And in the synagogue the only power is learning and the only riches prayer.

The Shabbat is different, too, because it is the day of rest not only for man but for his servants and his animals. On that day the ox is not worked and the horse

A COMMANDMENT OF GOD

God commanded the Jews to do their work in six days and to rest on the Sabbath. A Jew shows that he personally accepts the Covenant by obeying this Commandment.

is not ridden, the sheep is not sheared. When the Shabbat is truly observed, the entire world seems to be at peace—at least for that day.

A home holiday

For almost two thousand years now, the most important Shabbat observance is in the home. Every Jewish home became a *mikdash me'at,* a little sanctuary; the parents are the priests and the family table is the altar.

Long ago, as in Jewish homes today, the Shabbat was first the mother's. She prepared for it all through Friday, cleaning the house for Shabbat, cooking the Shabbat feast, bathing the children, getting the entire family dressed in their best clothes. Just before sundown she dropped coins into the charity box that stood in the kitchen. Then she lit the Shabbat candles.

Today, when many Shabbat customs are forgotten, lighting the Shabbat candles is the most observed home ritual.

Shabbat blessings

As the sun goes down on Friday evening, the mother lights the candles and recites the blessing:

וְצִוָּנוּ לְהַדְלִיק נֵר שֶׁל־שַׁבָּת:

and commanded us to light the Shabbat candles.

Then the father of the house blesses his children, "May the Lord make thee as Ephraim and Manasseh," for boys, and "May the Lord make thee as Sarah, Rebecca, Rachel, and Leah," for girls. Because he is the head of a family in a nation of priests, the father recites the priestly blessing over his children:

May the Lord bless thee and keep thee.
May the Lord cause His countenance to shine upon thee and be gracious unto thee,
May the Lord lift up His countenance unto thee and give thee peace. Amen.

In honor of his wife, the father recites from Proverbs the *Eshet Ḥayil*, a woman of valor. (See Chapter 6.)

More important than any single part of this ritual is its spirit. A father—not some outside person, however holy—blesses the children. The mother is praised by her husband for being the center, the foundation, of the family. Together, in their own home, parents and children move together, become united in love. As if they were close together in the Hand of God. And the peace of Shabbat descends upon them. The home may be poor or rich or in between, the days before may have been filled with trouble, there may have been quarrels within the family—but in that Shabbat ceremony, there is peace and kindness and love.

The Shabbat dinner

The Shabbat table is covered with the best tablecloth, set with the best dishes, with the silver *Kiddush* cup, and with two *ḥallot*. In the old days the best tablecloths were always white. Today, we use the best, whatever color, for this is the celebration meal of the best day.

The Kiddush cup doesn't have to be silver. Any glass will do—except that this is the special meal of the special day and the wine is one of its special symbols. So we try to get a special cup.

And in the old days, an everyday meal had one main dish and one loaf of bread went with it. Feasts of celebration had two main dishes, so there were two loaves of bread. The Shabbat meal is a feast—so there are two ḥallot.

The Rabbis gave a reason from the Bible. When the Jews escaped from Egypt and were wandering in the wilderness, God caused manna to fall from the sky for them to eat. On Friday, God caused a double portion of manna to fall so the Jews would not have to work gathering it on the Shabbat. So there are two ḥallot to remind us of the double portion of manna.

יוֹם הַשִּׁשִּׁי: וַיְכֻלּוּ הַשָּׁמַיִם
וְהָאָרֶץ. וְכָל־צְבָאָם...
בָּרוּךְ אַתָּה יי אֱלֹהֵינוּ
מֶלֶךְ הָעוֹלָם בּוֹרֵא פְּרִי
הַגָּפֶן... וְשַׁבַּת קָדְשְׁךָ
בְּאַהֲבָה וּבְרָצוֹן הִנְחַלְתָּנוּ
בָּרוּךְ אַתָּה יי
מְקַדֵּשׁ
הַשַּׁבָּת:

חַלָּה

The ḥallah bread gets its name from an offering to God that goes back to Bible times. When the housewife baked bread, she put aside a portion of it for the priests. This was called the *ḥallah portion.* Everyday bread was dark; bread for special occasions and for the priests was of white flour. Later eggs were added to the celebration breads and that is what makes our modern ḥallah so yellow. We also twist or braid the top—but this is not a rule.

As the family sits down to the Shabbat meal, the father recites the *Kiddush.* In ancient times every important meal began with a cup of wine. Even when this custom died out, and even when there was no wine for ordinary drinking, the cup of wine opening the Shabbat meal was kept. The Kiddush is more than a blessing over the wine. After the blessing:

בּוֹרֵא פְּרִי הַגָּפֶן

who creates the fruit of the vine

comes a long blessing which is really for the Sabbath day. We remember the creation and the Exodus from Egypt and bless God for giving us the Sabbath.

Kiddush over wine is also said in the synagogue on Friday night. In the old days the synagogue was the real center of the community of Jews. There were no hotels and the rough inns were no place for a Jew. So travelers who had no other place to stay were put up in the synagogue or in rooms attached to it. And the Kiddush for the Sabbath was so important that it was said at the service for everyone. We no longer put up strangers in our synagogues, but we remind ourselves

SABBATH AT HOME

Jews celebrate the Sabbath with joy and beauty, with love and charity. The mother lights the candles. The father blesses the children and recites a poem in praise of women. Kiddush is said. Then the family enjoys the special Sabbath meal, bound together in love—for each other and for God.

TIME TO BE TOGETHER

The Sabbath gives families time to be together. Fathers have time for their children. The family may go visiting or have company, go for walks, read, study, or rest.

of the laws of hospitality by still singing the Kiddush in the synagogue.

The Shabbat meal really begins when the father uncovers a ḥallah, cuts it, recites the blessing:

הַמּוֹצִיא לֶחֶם מִן־הָאָרֶץ

who brings forth bread from the earth

and gives a piece to each person at the table. The ḥallah is covered until this moment because in ancient days the bread was not brought to the table until after Kiddush was said. In later days the table was set completely before the candles were lit; the ḥallah was covered as if it weren't there at all. It appears as soon as the covering is taken off.

The Rabbis have a religious reason for this, too. They said that every symbol of the Shabbat is equally important. If the ḥallah was on the table while the Kiddush was said, it would look as if wine was more important than bread. By covering the ḥallah during the Kiddush, then uncovering it for its blessing, we give it equal importance with the wine.

Families in Eastern Europe—from whom most American Jews are descended—used to have both fish and meat for their Shabbat meal. The fish was usually stuffed *(gefilte)* fish. But there's no religious reason for any particular food on the Sabbath. It was gefilte fish and chicken for many years because this was the best food they had. So, too, today, we eat the most enjoyable food during the Shabbat meal in recognition of the fact that this is a joyful day.

Customs and services

After the Shabbat meal, the family sat around the table singing *zemirot,* happy songs in praise of the Shabbat and of God who gave this holiday to the Jews.

There was another feature of the Shabbat meal, as important as all the rest. This was the Shabbat guest. At services, members of the congregation kept an eye out for a poor man, for a student, for a stranger, to invite home for the Shabbat meal. It made the feast holier, more joyful, in keeping with the spirit of the day. Sometimes there were not enough poor students or strangers to go around and there would be competition for a guest because no one wanted his Shabbat table to look as if he lacked charity.

Shabbat morning, the entire family went to services in the synagogue. This was the most important service of the week in the synagogue. Since no one had to go to work there was time for more prayers, for reading a long Torah portion, and a portion from the Prophets. As the services ended, everyone turned to his neighbor with the traditional Shabbat greeting, *"gut Shabbos,"* or *"Shabbat shalom"*—good or peaceful Shabbat.

Shabbat afternoon was spent visiting relatives, studying, taking a walk, even napping—all quite different from the everyday—and so special to Shabbat. A favorite way of spending the afternoon in the spring and summer was for the father to study a chapter of the *Pirké Avot,* the *Sayings of the Fathers,* with his sons. Since *Avot* talks about right and wrong, correct ways and incorrect, it is a proper subject for study on the Shabbat. Many fathers also used the Shabbat as a time to see what their children had been studying in their Jewish school all week.

The end of the Sabbath

When three stars appear, marking the end of the Shabbat, the father takes wine, spices, and a special braided

candle and says the *Havdalah* (separation) blessings. There are four of them after an introduction made up of happy Bible verses. The youngest child usually holds the Havdalah candle. The father lights it. Then he says the regular blessing over the wine. Then over the spices *(Besamim)* in their special spicebox (besamim box):

> בּוֹרֵא מִינֵי בְשָׂמִים:
> *who creates the different spices.*

Then over the candle:

> בּוֹרֵא מְאוֹרֵי הָאֵשׁ:
> *who creates the lights of fire.*

Then the separation blessing. Its main words are:

> הַמַּבְדִּיל בֵּין־קֹדֶשׁ לְחֹל. בֵּין־אוֹר לְחֹשֶׁךְ:
> *who divides the holy from the ordinary, the light from the darkness.*

שָׁבוּעַ טוֹב

The Shabbat is then over and the week has begun. People often sing *Eliyahu ha-Navi,* "Elijah the Prophet," and *Shavua Tov,* "A Good Week."

A day for sharing

The Shabbat is also the day on which the family shares its joys and sorrows with the congregation. If a child was born, the father was called to the Torah and special prayers were said for mother and child. If it was a girl child, she was given her name in the synagogue on the first Shabbat. When a boy turned 13, he had his Bar Mitzvah ceremony in the synagogue on the Shabbat. On the Shabbat before a wedding, the groom was called to the Torah in the synagogue. When a Jew escaped great danger or recovered from a serious illness, he came to the synagogue on the Shabbat and recited the *ha-Gomel* blessing, "God is benevolent, even to the undeserving." On the first Shabbat after a burial, the family came to the synagogue to be comforted. And if a Jew was wronged by another Jew, he could inter-

SHARING IN THE SYNAGOGUE

At the Sabbath synagogue service people hear of and share in important events that concern each other: a coming wedding, the naming of a baby, prayers of thanks for recovery from illness or escape from danger. They rejoice with the happy and help comfort the sad.

rupt the Shabbat service to ask for justice. Whatever was important to the individual was shared with the community of Jews on the Shabbat.

These were the old customs, the traditional Shabbat customs, the customs our grandparents and great-grandparents knew and followed. They are still followed by many Jews throughout the world; even where not all these practices are followed, some Shabbat customs are practiced by almost all Jews. And each has meaning even in the very modern Shabbat.

Need for Sabbath today

In the ancient days, when most people worked desperately hard all day every day, one day of rest in every seven was a very radical idea—and a great joy. Today, everyone gets at least one day, often two days, away from work every week. But most people spend these days, not in rest, but in a different kind of busyness—sometimes a busyness of pleasure. That doesn't teach us much about what it means to be a real person. It doesn't stop all the rush and bother of the week and get us to ask where we are going and why, or what we are doing with our time to help the Jewish people bring the Days of the Messiah. The Jewish Shabbat is still different—and necessary. Every seven days we need to step out of our usual routine so we can remember that we are servants of God and not slaves of men.

9

Every day

There are 365 days in a regular year. But there are fewer than a hundred Sabbaths, feast days, fast days and holidays in a Jewish year. We could say that the year has more ordinary days than special days—except that for Jews there are no ordinary days. In a way, every day is a holy day for Jews. That is one of the ways Jews deal with time.

The special days have special ways of marking them, of celebrating what they stand for. But marking these days—by going to the synagogue, by holding a feast, by observing the ceremonies—is not all there is to being religious. Not if by being religious we mean being someone who believes in God, has faith in God, and tries to follow God's laws.

Saying and doing—every day

Judaism does not measure a Jew only by what he does in the synagogue—no matter how loudly he prays and how carefully he follows all the customs and rituals. Being a Jew depends as much on what a person does at home, in business, in school, on the street. Being a

EACH DAY HOLY

Each day is a gift from God. Every day is holy as we remember and obey God's laws. A Jew has the spirit of his prayers with him throughout the day. He listens to the inner voice that tells him what is right or wrong. He remembers God, too, in saying blessings for good things, in being pleasant to others, by holding back harsh words, by doing deeds of kindness and charity, by standing up against wrongdoing.

good Jew means serving God at all times, every day. And there are more "every days" than holidays.

We all know children who are like angels when being watched, and like devils when on their own.

We all know young people who are just perfect when teachers or other adults are around, and as mean as they can be when with their own age group.

We all know adults who weep loudly on Yom Kippur as they read the list of sins and then continue to commit the same sins all the rest of the year.

Every day holy

This is not the way of Judaism. To a Jew, every day is a holy day because God exists every day, not just on holidays; because every day is like a new creation of His for us. The prayer book says, "In His goodness He renews the work of creation each day, continually." Every morning it is as if the world is created anew, and as if every person were born afresh.

So when we get up in the morning we have some special things to do to show that we are Jews and appreciate God's gift of the new day. Each day is begun with thanks for being alive and blessings that we are well. Then, traditionally, a Jew goes to the synagogue for *Shaḥarit* (morning) prayers. There, the first thing he does is put on his *Tallit* (prayer shawl) and his *Tefillin* (phylacteries).

Keeping God's law

תְּפִילִין

שֶׁל רֹאשׁ

שֶׁל יָד

The Bible tells us that we must keep God's laws in our hearts at all times, teach them to our children and "bind them for a sign upon thy hand, and they shall be for frontlets between thine eyes." Traditionally the Tefillin are a daily reminder to remember and keep the laws that God gave us—which will give us, in turn, a good life. That's why they are not worn on Shabbat and festivals—those special days are reminders enough.

Tefillin are two leather boxes in which are placed pieces of parchment on which are written verses from the Torah. One, called *Shel Rosh* (of the head), is placed on the forehead. The other, *Shel Yad* (of the arm), is tied to the upper left arm, close to the heart. The leather thong that ties the *Shel Yad* is wrapped seven times around the arm, three times around the middle finger, and the rest about the palm.

A boy begins to put on ("lay") Tefillin when he becomes Bar Mitzvah. In some communities of Jews the first "laying" of Tefillin in the synagogue is the most important Bar Mitzvah ceremony. For all its beauty, the wearing of Tefillin has been given up by many Jews.

Morning prayers

The morning prayers in the synagogue today include most of the private prayers that used to be said at home by each person on arising. These are blessings and prayers of thanks. The regular daily morning service begins with psalms and then includes the many prayers you know from going to synagogue. On Mondays and Thursdays, a portion of the Torah is read.

There are still many traditional Jews who go to morning services every day. But even the people who do not go to daily synagogue services say some form of prayer at home.

All day long the idea of the prayers will go along with the Jew: when he says the special blessings for

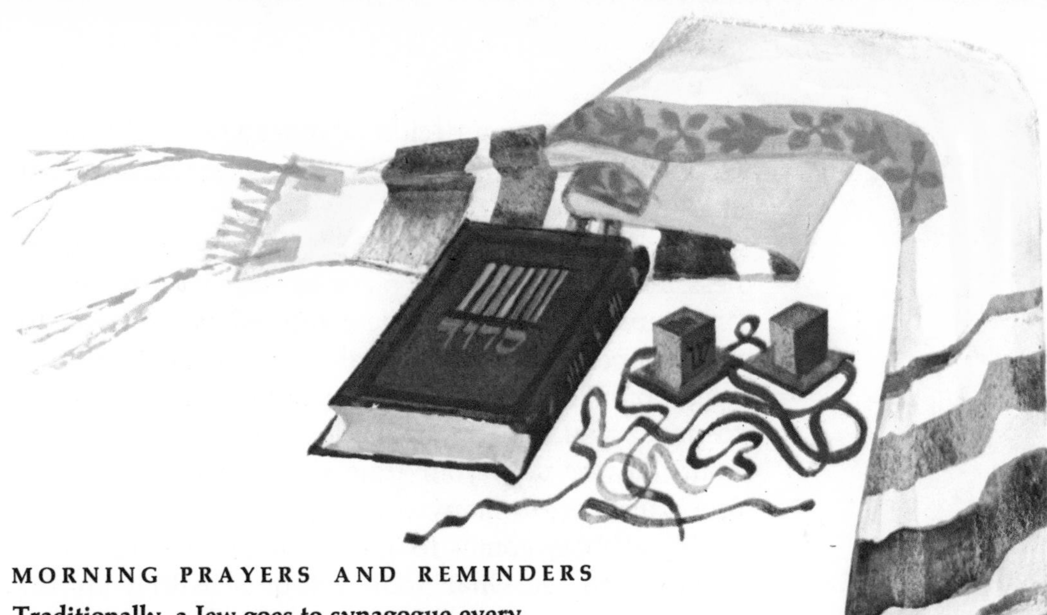

MORNING PRAYERS AND REMINDERS

Traditionally, a Jew goes to synagogue every morning. There, before his morning prayers, he binds on phylacteries, Tefillin, as reminders of God's laws.

things that come his way; when he smiles at a stranger; when he does an act of charity; when he stands up against wrongdoing; when he scatters some crumbs for birds; when he holds back a harsh word. Then, dozens of times every day, he shows what a Jew does with his time and he makes holy even an ordinary day.

Ways of goodness

Some teachers have tried to make lists of mitzvot that would cover everything we might do during the day. But no one can make rules about everything. So along with their rules the Rabbis gave us teachings—about mercy and justice, about love and understanding, about goodness and courage. When we go through the day we try to live not just by the Jewish rules but also by the Jewish teachings. And that is one reason why Jewish schools are so important in Judaism.

So what a Jew takes with him wherever he goes all day is a mood, a feeling about doing good. It is a kind of radar inside that helps you find out right from wrong. It helps you decide whether you are following God or not. With this sense inside us we can serve God at all times.

How can we learn enough to have a radar for goodness inside us? The best place to start is to remember one commandment, the one Rabbi Akiva said was the most important in the Torah: "Thou shalt love thy neighbor as thyself." It is so simple to say; it is so hard to do. If you will try to make it your guide hour by hour, day by day, your time will be full of goodness and a blessing to many.

As each day comes to an end there are things to do to help you see what you have done with your day. One comes as the workday is over, the other comes when you go to sleep.

Evening prayers

מִנְחָה
מַעֲרִיב

In Bible days, there were two main services in the Temple, the morning, or *Shaḥarit,* service and the afternoon, or *Minḥah,* service. In the synagogue, too, there is a Minḥah service and an evening service called *Ma'ariv,* from the first words of the opening blessing ("who brings on the evening twilight").

Since most men would find it hard to leave their work and go to the synagogue three times a day, the afternoon and evening services were combined into a Minḥah-Ma'ariv service, which takes place immediately before and immediately after the sun goes down.

Like daily morning prayers, Minḥah and Ma'ariv are not said in every synagogue. Some Jews, and children particularly, content themselves with bedtime prayers, of which there are many. This is a time for thinking about the day gone by, and how we used it, and of the new day that will be with us when we wake. We close the day saying the Shema as a pledge to God and a promise to His people.

EVENING PRAYERS

In his evening prayers, at synagogue or at home, a Jew gives thanks to God for the day. Even little children say bedtime prayers. They can think about the day that is past and the new day to come. They recite the Shema as a pledge to God.

Living each day

So every day, from getting up to going to sleep, has its special religious acts. They are not celebrations but they turn just another day to another chance to serve God and make the world what it ought to be. Because we do that day after day after day our Sabbaths can mean more to us. Because our weekdays and our Sabbaths come to mean so much to us we know they will bring all men to the Days of the Messiah.

THE MONTHS

A week is a short seven days.
A year is a long, long time.
To divide the time in between, most people have
months.

Months are moons.
For some people it is exactly the time from one new
moon to another.
Roughly that time for others.
For the Jews,
The unending, unchanging cycle of moon to moon
Is a great wonder,
And a sign of God's goodness.

But the months—which follow the moon's movement
about the earth—
And the years—which follow the earth's movement
about the sun—
Do not fit together smoothly.
You cannot divide the year into a whole number of
moons.
But our forefathers found a way of arranging a
calendar
That measured both.

It is our Jewish way of adding
days, and
weeks, and
months
To get years of goodness,
That move the years steadily forward toward the
Kingdom of God.

10

The Jewish calendar

Jewish holidays stand on two legs, one in heaven and one on this earth. They cannot be divided. Take God out of any Jewish holiday and you take away one of its two legs—and it falls flat.

Days of remembrance

Ḥanukkah celebrates a victory in a war. So does Patriots' Day, which you probably have never heard of unless you live in Massachusetts. Ḥanukkah celebrates the retaking of Jerusalem by the Maccabees. Patriots' Day marks the victory of the Americans at the Battle of Lexington. But if the Jews were to celebrate Ḥanukkah only because of the victory of the Maccabees over the Syrians, the holiday would be only as important—and as little-remembered—as Patriots' Day. Ḥanukkah is celebrated today with joy and feasting and prayer, exactly as it has been for two thousand years. Ḥanukkah is as important today as it was a thousand years ago because it celebrates not only victory in a war, but the reason for that war: the Jews' willingness to die rather than to give up their God. Ḥanukkah belongs half to the Jews and half to God.

Pesaḥ celebrates the Jews' escape to freedom, the beginning of the Jews as a nation. In much the same way, July 4 is Independence Day for Americans. Yet how many Americans really use the Fourth of July holiday as a day of remembrance? But Jews celebrate Pesaḥ today much as their forefathers did, with the same words and the same ceremonies. Pesaḥ has the same observance now that it did a thousand years ago because of its religious meaning.

It's the same with Rosh Hashanah. Without its message of repentance and a new beginning it would be another New Year's Eve—without the parties.

So Jewish holidays last, and are important, because they mark not only what the Jews did, but God's place in Jewish history. The events marked by the holidays belong to this world; the idea of the holiday comes from God.

The Talmud says the holidays were decided upon by God. But since some months were made long and some short, God left it to man to decide the exact day that year on which the holiday would be celebrated.

How do we decide on which particular day to celebrate Rosh Hashanah? or Pesaḥ? or Shavuot? or the other feast days and fast days? In other words, how do we Jews measure time?

Counting days

Counting days is easy. The sun tells us when a day is completed and the next day begins. A day is from sundown to sundown, or from sunup to sunup. The modern world marks the day from midnight to midnight. It is more convenient in a world of factories and schools and banks to change from Monday to

WHY THE JEWISH CALENDAR?

A calendar counts time. It keeps count of the Holy Days and Festivals on the days God commanded. Jews count days from sundown to sundown. Weeks are seven days long, from Sabbath to Sabbath. Jewish months are counted from the coming of one new moon to the next—29½ days. So one Jewish month has 29 days and the next 30.

Tuesday, from Tuesday to Wednesday when most people are asleep. But in the ancient world people worked with the sun and rested when it got dark. The day ended when the sun went down. So the Jewish calendar has its days from sundown to sundown. As long as anyone can remember, all Jews, everywhere, have used this system for their religion. This is in keeping with the Biblical verse, "and it was evening, and it was morning . . ."

Counting months and years

Once you go beyond days, the counting becomes a bit harder. However, even primitive man noticed two things that happened time after time after time. The moon appeared, filled, grew smaller, and disappeared about every 29½ days. That's where the idea of months, "moons," came from. And the sun returned to exactly the same position in the sky every 365¼ days (actually, its 365 days, 5 hours, 48 minutes, 45½ seconds). That's where we get years.

MOON MONTHS AND SUN YEARS

Farming follows the seasons of the sun. The sun year is measured by the return of the sun to the same place in the sky. It is 365 ¼ + days long. There are more than 12 moon months, plus an extra 11 days, in a sun year of 365 days.

The trouble is, they don't come out even. If you tried to divide 29½ into 365¼ you'd get a remainder. Twelve moon months don't make one sun year. That's bad because the seasons go according to the sun, cold in winter when the sun is low; hot in summer when the sun is high.

It's a problem for the Muslims who keep time according to the moon. They have twelve moon months every year—adding up to 354 days. But that's eleven days less than a sun year with 365 days. So every year the Muslim calendar slips back eleven days. A Muslim child born in the middle of April has his first birthday in the beginning of April, his second birthday in March. His birthday comes in the winter when he's about 10 years old, and in the fall when he's a teenager. Not until he's grown up does his birthday come back to mid-April.

Fixing the calendar

In early Bible days when the Hebrews were shepherds, they counted time by the moon. As more and more of them became farmers they had to keep time with the seasons. They had to know when they could start putting their seeds into the ground. They developed a sun-year calendar to keep the months in their proper seasons.

So the Jewish calendar uses a little of the moon method and of the sun method of counting time. A month is a moon month—29½ days; two moon months are 59 days. So Jews normally have one month of 29 days, followed by one month of 30 days.

That still left the problem of combining moon months and sun years. The Bible commands the Children of Israel to celebrate Pesaḥ during the month in which barley ripens. (To be exact, on the fifteenth day of Nisan.) Shavuot, the festival of the first fruits, comes exactly 50 days later. And Sukkot, the festival of the fall harvest, comes exactly 145 days later.

If Jews only counted moon months, Pesaḥ would soon move back into the winter. While it might be called the fifteenth of Nisan, the barley wouldn't even be planted, let alone ready for harvest. Shavuot wouldn't have any first fruits, and Sukkot would be in midsummer, long before the harvest.

In the early years, the priests would not announce the date of Pesaḥ until they had sent messengers into the country to see how the grain was doing. If the barley wasn't ripening, if the lambs were too small, Pesaḥ was put off for a month. This gave the year an extra month—13 moons instead of 12. The Jewish leap year doesn't add just a day but a whole month! This extra month is put in right after the month of Adar and so it is called *Adar Sheni*, Second Adar. The Jewish leap year is longer than a sun year. The way it was worked out, one came every two or three years, seven times in every 19 years. And although most of the months are about at the same season year after year, the sun and moon calendars are exactly equal every 19 years. A Jewish holiday in 1971 will fall on the same date in the general sun calendar in 1990 and 2009. You can see why even in olden times Jews studied arithmetic and astronomy.

Fixing the holidays

Having fixed the calendar, the Jews were faced with another problem. This time the problem had to do with human beings. If Yom Kippur, a fast day, came on Friday or Sunday—the day before or the day after the Sabbath—the people would suffer. If Yom Kippur fell on Friday, there would be no time to prepare food for the Sabbath. And if Yom Kippur fell on Sunday, there would be no time to prepare a hot meal to carry the people over the fast day because cooking is forbidden on the Sabbath.

So the rule is that Rosh Hashanah, the day from which other holidays are counted, may not fall on a Sunday, a Wednesday, or a Friday—thus making it impossible for Yom Kippur to fall on Friday or Sunday. In years in which the regular Jewish calendar would put Rosh Hashanah on one of those days, an extra day is added—or a day is subtracted. If a day is added, it is put into *Ḥeshvan,* the next month. If a day is subtracted, it is taken from *Kislev,* the month after that.

Naming the days and months

Among most peoples, days and months have names—usually the names of gods or heavenly things. Sunday is named after the sun, Monday after the moon; Thursday is named after Thor, Friday after Freyia, two Scandinavian gods. January is named after Janus, a Roman god, March after Mars, July after Julius Caesar, August after Augustus, the Roman emperor who considered himself a god.

Jewish days do not have names—except for the seventh day which is Shabbat. Sunday is the First Day (of the week), Monday is Second Day, Friday is the day before Sabbath.

NAMES OF DAYS AND MONTHS

The days and months of the Jewish calendar are not named for pagan gods or heavenly bodies. The days of the Jewish week are numbered—except for Shabbat. Jewish months were first named from the kind of work done in them. But since the exile in Babylon they have had Babylonian names.

The Hebrews in Bible days did have names for the months, but these came from the work done during the month. There was olive-harvest month, grain-planting month, fig-harvest month, vine-tending month, and so on. But when the ancient Jews lived in Babylon (after the destruction of the First Temple), they adopted the Babylonian names for the months. We still use those names.

Set-up of the calendar

If you start with the Rosh Hashanah month, this is how our Jewish calendar is set up:

It took some time before this was the calendar. Before that, people only knew it would be a new month when the new moon appeared. So they kept watch for the changes in the sky. Then they learned a little astronomy and could pretty well tell when the new moon would appear. They still kept watchmen on the hills to report the heavenly changes. When the new moon appeared, and the month was begun officially, they would send out a signal. The watchmen would light fires on the hilltop or blow the shofar. Someone on the next hilltop would repeat the signal and so on.

Later a messenger system was used. This worked fine —so long as most of the Jews lived in the Land of Israel. When Jews lived all over the Middle East and around the Mediterranean Sea, the messengers took a long time getting there and the people at a distance couldn't follow the calendar easily.

To make sure the holidays were celebrated on the proper days, the Rabbis said that all Biblical holidays except fast days should be celebrated for two days outside Palestine. So the seven-day celebration of Pesaḥ became eight days outside of Palestine. The eight-day Sukkot became nine days. Shavuot became two days. But fast days, like Yom Kippur, remained one day because forty-eight hours of fasting might be too much for some people. In Israel only Rosh Hashanah is observed for two days. Most Reform Jews in America also keep only one day of the holidays, including only one day of Rosh Hashanah.

That light in the night sky that appears as a thin sliver one evening, grows larger every day until it is a great round ball, then slowly disappears was a source of wonder and awe to every people. To them, as to the ancient Hebrews, it was an important way of telling time. So for many peoples, the appearance of the new moon was a time for special celebration.

The beginning of the month

From the earliest times, and to this day, all Jewish holidays are counted from the new moon, from *Rosh Ḥodesh,* "the beginning of the month." In the days of the Temple in Jerusalem, the High Priest appeared before the people in his golden robes only on Shabbat, on holidays, and on Rosh Ḥodesh. It was a small Rosh

Hashanah, a beginning in time. Each month was God's gift. It was a new chance, so Jews were happy and grateful to Him.

To this day Rosh Ḥodesh is a kind of holiday, but its celebration has become quite small.

On the Shabbat that comes immediately before the appearance of the new moon we say a prayer that the new month may bring us blessings. In the synagogue, on Rosh Ḥodesh, special psalms are said and the Torah is read. When the new moon actually appears, a special blessing is said, looking at the moon.

Rosh Ḥodesh used to be a half holiday in Jewish schools, but that custom has almost disappeared. And this day was celebrated as a special holiday for women. It isn't any longer, though in some Orthodox homes women do not sew or do other work that can be put off on Rosh Ḥodesh.

ROSH ḤODESH

In Temple times, the day when the new moon appeared was a special holiday on which the High Priest wore his golden robes. Later Rosh Ḥodesh was a kind of half holiday. Even now some Orthodox women put off unnecessary work on that day. The Jewish calendar binds the people together. All over the world they greet the New Year, celebrate the Seder on the same day. The calendar binds Jews to God in helping build a better world.

The beginning of the year

In order to count the days and months of the year, you have to have a place to begin. Where do you begin the year? Most early peoples began their years with the spring when everything came alive once again. But some people began in the fall, others in midwinter. The Jews gave their year several beginnings! Rosh Hashanah, which you probably know as the beginning of the year, doesn't come on the first day of the first month. The Bible designates it as the first day of the seventh month, Tishri; Nisan is the first month, marking the beginning of spring.

The Mishnah, the first great compilation of Oral Law, says that the first day of the month of Nisan shall begin the new year for kings. The years of the reign of the kings of Israel were counted from this day. The first of Tishri, says the Mishnah, shall be the religious new year and the date for the number of the year to be changed.

There is still another new year, *Ḥamishah Asar bi-Shevat* (or Tu bi-Shevat), the fifteenth day of Shevat. This is the New Year of the Trees, marking the time when the sap first begins to rise in the fruit trees in Israel. Since the Torah tells the Jews not to eat from their fruit trees for several years after they are planted, this date is the birthday for all of them.

Now you can see how the days lead into the weeks, the weeks are tied together to become months, and the months are added together to make years. It is all part of the Jewish hope to tie time to God, to help every man link his life with his people and God, to build a world of peace and love and justice.

THE SEASONS

The Jewish year is 50 or 55 weeks,
But you can't tell what week it is by looking outside.
The Jewish year is 12 or 13 months,
But you can't tell the name of the month by how it feels.
You can tell what season it is,
Which of the four seasons of the year.

When the days are short and the nights long,
When the air is cold and snow is likely every day,
It is a sign of winter.

When the days grow longer and the air warms,
When the earth itself begins to move and grow,
It is a sign of spring.

When night holds off till bedtime,
And the days are too warm for work and school,
It is summer.

When there's a new crispness in the air,
And the leaves turn and school begins again,
It is autumn.

Again the night creeps into the daytime,
The snow threatens.
The year has come full circle and it is winter again.

So the year turns, year after year.
And each year we mark the seasons—
Each season means something new to us.
Each season means something old to our people.

11

Spring: Passover

Very early in our history, the Jews were slaves. With God's help, they won their way out of slavery and into freedom. The experience of being slaves and of the struggling for freedom taught the Jews that all men must be free if they are truly to be men. Then, and later, the Jews also learned that there is no true freedom unless all men are free. So for Jews, serving God means trying to achieve freedom for all men.

A springtime celebration

For most people spring is the time of new crops. It is a promise that they will have a fine harvest—so they celebrate.

For Jews too the new growing things are a great joy and they thank God for them. But it is also the time of freedom. So Passover (Pesaḥ) is a double celebration: the Feast of Unleavened Bread, and also our springtime Festival of Freedom. It is the holiday of spring, a celebration of what happens in nature. And it is the holiday of an historical event, a celebration of how God brought us from Egyptian slavery to freedom. Every year it reminds us that no man is truly free as long as another man is in chains—real chains, or chains of fear, or chains of hunger, or chains of prejudice. Pesaḥ comes every year to celebrate that we are free from winter. Once again the out-of-doors opens to us. Once again we can plant and grow things. We rejoice over nature; we celebrate our history.

Scholars think that long before the Jews went down into Egypt, while they were still shepherds, the first Jews celebrated the coming of spring. It was the season when kids and lambs are born, when the new grass came through that the animals might eat. So on the night of the spring full moon (generally the 15th of Nisan, the first spring month), they roasted a lamb and feasted on the meat in celebration.

When the Jews settled in Canaan they became farmers, and spring became more important. They wanted the earth to open to their seed and make it grow.

The first Passover

Then came a time of famine, when there was nothing to eat. Except in Egypt. As the Bible tells us, the Pharaohs welcomed the Jews and then enslaved them. But God would not let His people stay in slavery.

God sent ten plagues. The rivers ran blood, frogs filled the wells, insects covered the people. Cattle died, there came boils, hail, locusts, darkness. Still Pharaoh was stubborn. Then came the last plague, the death of the first-born.

The last plague came on the night of the old spring festival, of the lamb sacrifice. And the Jews marked their doorposts with the blood of the sacrifice so the Angel of Death would *pass over* their houses. (*Pesaḥ* may be understood as the Hebrew word for "pass

SPRINGTIME AND FREEDOM

Passover is a festival of spring. And it is a festival of freedom and deliverance. It celebrates the Jews' coming out of Egypt. When God punished the Egyptians with the plague, the Jews marked their doorposts with the blood of lambs sacrificed at the spring festival. And the angel of death passed over their houses.

over.") That night the Jews hurriedly left Egypt—so quickly, the Bible says, the dough for the next day's bread was unleavened. When they came to the Sea of Reeds and Pharaoh sent his armies after them, the sea opened. The Jews crossed, and Pharaoh's armies were destroyed. That is how, scholars think, the old spring sacrifice of the lamb became also the festival of freedom, of escape from slavery.

סֵדֶר

In most religions, the important ceremonies take place in a church or mosque or shrine. Among Jews the celebrations are divided between synagogue and home. On Pesaḥ the observance called *Seder*, "order" of ceremonies, takes place in the home. It is a family feast of remembrance and thanksgiving.

The Haggadah

Four times the Bible commands the Jews to celebrate Pesaḥ in a very special way: "You shall tell your son on that day and say: We celebrate because of what the

Lord did for me when I came forth out of Egypt" (Exodus 13). This commandment requires every Jew, in every age, in every place, to remind his children on the Seder night how they became free and why they should love freedom. Note that the Torah says "when I came forth." Not those Jews then but we Jews now were, in a way, slaves and now are free. So every Jew must tell his children how *they* were slaves and *their* slavery was bitter, and God brought *them* forth out of slavery.

הַגָּדָה

In Hebrew the telling is *Haggadah,* and that is where we get the name for the book we use at the Seder. It is not only a telling of history but of explanations, fables, legends, stories, prayers, songs.

The Haggadah is very old. Parts of it were set down well before the time of the Maccabees. From the records of about 1,800 years ago we know the Haggadah then was pretty much as it is now.

Of course, some changes did take place with time. At the time the Temple was destroyed, the Haggadah included only three questions for the child to ask. One question asked about unleavened bread, one about dipping herbs, and one asked, "On all other nights, we eat meat roasted, stewed, or cooked [boiled]; why on this night only roasted?" When the Temple was de-

OLD AND NEW HAGGADOT

The Bible commands that a father tell his children on Passover eve the story of the Jews' coming out of slavery in Egypt. The traditional Haggadah tells this Bible story, with Rabbinical explanations, fables, legends, prayers, and songs. Newer Haggadot include recent attempts by tyrants to oppress the Jews.

stroyed, and sacrifices, which were roasts, ended, it no longer made sense to ask about eating only roasted meat. So that question was dropped and the one asking about leaning while eating was put in. Later, a fourth question, about bitter herbs, was added.

New Haggadot

Since Pesaḥ is a family celebration, it is very important that everyone at the Seder understand what is being said. So Haggadot were translated into almost every language spoken by Jews. There was even a Latin translation in 1512. But perhaps the greatest additions to the Haggadah in recent centuries came after the end of World War II. There was the death of six million Jews, the deliverance from Nazism, the establishment of the State of Israel. This was a new slavery, a new exodus from slavery, a new journey to the Promised Land. So many people added new parts to their Haggadot, reciting the twentieth-century victory over tyranny. There are today many different Haggadot which try to give the Seder special meaning to certain groups of Jews.

So long as the story is taught to the children, the blessings are said, and the symbols discussed—so long as every person at the Seder understands that he personally was freed from slavery—it is still the same Passover celebration.

The Great Sabbath

In the synagogue, preparation for Pesaḥ begins before the holiday comes. The Shabbat immediately before the first Seder is called *Shabbat ha-Gadol,* the Great Sabbath. It is so called because the Haftarah portion which is read on that day is from the Biblical book of Malachi 3:4–24. It speaks of the time when Elijah will be sent to announce the "great day of the Lord."

Some say this Shabbat got its name because people gathered in the synagogue on the Shabbat before

Pesaḥ to listen to a lecture on observing the holiday. The speaker was the *greatest* authority; and he spoke for the *greatest* time.

Passover kindnesses

מָעוֹת חִטִּים

Another sort of preparation has to do with the commandment that a Jew feed the hungry and the unfortunate—at all times. On Pesaḥ, the poor too must have special Passover food. In Europe, the rabbi and two leading members of the congregation would go from house to house during the weeks before Pesaḥ, collecting money. This money—*maot ḥittim,* or money for wheat (*matzah*)—was given to the poor so they could buy food for Pesaḥ. Today, in larger communities, we still have maot ḥittim funds, and there is always a special effort to see that Jews away from home in colleges, hospitals, or the armed forces will be able to celebrate a Seder.

No leavened bread

To make bread, ordinary bread, yeast or some other leavening is added to the dough. This makes the dough rise, expand; it takes several hours. But Jews didn't have hours when they left Egypt. In memory of the Exodus, Jews are commanded to "put all leaven out of"

HOLIDAY KINDNESSES

It is a mitzvah to celebrate the Passover, and a greater mitzvah to see to it that others can celebrate it. The Jewish community sees that every Jew has food at Pesaḥ and is able to celebrate the holiday. Money is collected for the poor. Travelers and students far from home are invited to share a family Seder.

our houses and to eat unleavened bread, *matzah*, during Pesaḥ.

To make sure there is no leaven—no material that will ferment, or turn sour—in the house, it is the Passover custom for Jews to clean their homes from top to bottom. It is like the spring house cleaning many people do. Special dishes, used only for Pesaḥ, are brought out and used during the holiday.

חָמֵץ

On the eve before Pesaḥ begins, the house is searched for food that might include leaven—*ḥametz*. But since the housewife has already cleaned the house thoroughly for the holiday, there's no ḥametz around. That gave rise to the practice of hiding little pieces of bread around the house. Then the father searches for them with a candle to see them by and a feather to sweep them up. The next morning they are taken outside and burned to show that the head of the household has fulfilled the commandment to cleanse his house of leaven.

Seder symbols

The Pesaḥ celebration really begins with the first Seder right after dark on the evening of the fifteenth of Nisan. The Seder does not have to be done by a priest or rabbi or specially trained man, but by the father, even if he is not particularly learned. Once again we practice the old Jewish teaching—all men are equal before God. The family gathers around the Seder table. It is covered by a lovely cloth and set with the special Pesaḥ dishes. Everyone is dressed up. The mood is gay and happy. Everyone has a Haggadah. There is also a wineglass for every person—including the children—and a special wineglass for the prophet Elijah. In front of the father's place are two special dishes. One is the Seder plate. On it are a roast lamb bone (*zeroa*), a roasted egg (*betzah*), bitter herbs (*maror*), greens (*karpas*), and a mixture of apples, nuts, wine (*ḥaroset*).

The maror, karpas, and ḥaroset are to be eaten. The

PASSOVER PREPARATIONS
The house is thoroughly cleaned before Passover and all leaven is removed from it. The Seder table is set with special china and glassware not used at other times.

zeroa and betzah are not. They are reminders. The lamb bone reminds us of the special Passover sacrifice, which was a lamb. The egg is a symbol of the regular holiday offerings made in the Temple. The Haggadah talks about the lamb bone but the roasted egg is a silent reminder.

To one side of the father's place at the Seder table is another plate. On it are three matzot, covered. Some say they represent the priests, their assistants, and the rest of the Jews, that is, the Kohanim, the Levites, and the regular Israelites. Another explanation is that on any festival we have two loaves of bread. So we need two matzot. But the Torah commands us to eat "the bread of slavery" at the Seder. It just doesn't seem right to call one of our two celebration matzot the bread of slavery, so a third is added.

During the Seder, every person will drink four cups of wine. The Rabbis said these four cups stand for the four ways in which God said He would bring the Jews out of slavery: He said, "I will bring you out . . . rid you of bondage . . . redeem you . . . take you to Me for a people." Two cups are drunk before the meal and the first of these is the holiday Kiddush. The other two are drunk after the meal. That is a real celebration indeed.

One other thing about the table. The father's chair has cushions or pillows on it. When free men feasted in ancient times they relaxed on sofas or benches covered with pillows. Slaves sat on hard stools—if they sat at all. So leaning back on cushions became a symbol of freedom. On Seder night, Jews lean on pillows to show that they are free. All the other days of the year may be filled with pain or hunger or oppression—but on this night every Jew is a free man and shows it.

Opening of the Seder

The Seder opens, as does every important Jewish festival, with the lighting of the candles and Kiddush over wine. But there is no Kiddush at the evening service in the synagogue before the Seder. It just couldn't happen that someone would not be either in his own home or a guest in another Jew's home for the Seder. So there is no need for a community Kiddush. (Usually the *Motzi* blessing comes after the Kiddush, but on Seder night there is a lot to say and think about before we eat so it comes later.)

After washing his hands, the father dips the karpas —usually celery or parsley or lettuce, but it can be any salad green—into salt water and gives each person at the table a piece. They all say the blessing:

בּוֹרֵא פְּרִי הָאֲדָמָה

who creates the fruit of the earth

and eat it. That is the very first special act of the Seder.

The fresh greens remind us that this is the Festival of Spring. Spring means that hope for a world of peace and of plenty is possible again. So we begin by celebrating the spring. But we dip the karpas in salt water to remind us of the tears our forefathers cried in slavery. We remember them as we remember the spring.

A FAMILY CEREMONY

The youngest child asks the four questions that lead his father to tell the Pesaḥ story. Everyone, family and guests, takes part in the ceremony as the father conducts it.

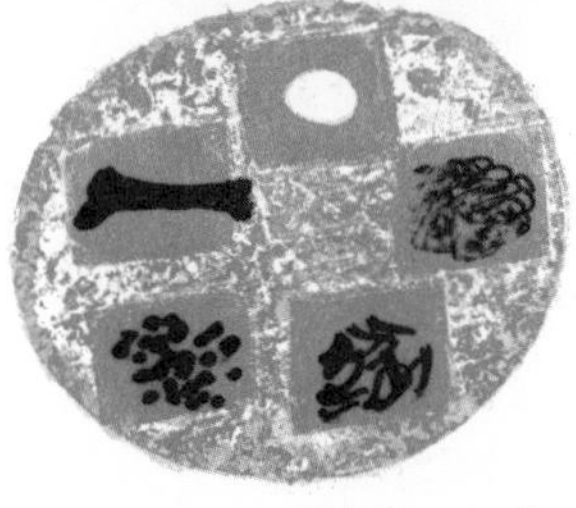

In this first special Pesaḥ act we bring together both ideas of the holiday.

Hiding the Afikoman

After everyone has eaten some karpas, the father breaks the middle matzah in two. One piece is set aside to be eaten at the close of the Seder. The name given this half piece of matzah—*afikoman*—is the best clue to its meaning.

When the Jews lived among the Greeks and Romans two thousand years ago, the fashionable thing to do was to go from one party to another, from one feast to another. This going from one party to another was called, in Greek, *epikomios.*

Young Jews who followed the Greek customs began to think of the Seder only as a feast, a party, and on the first night of Pesaḥ they went from one house to another. But the Seder is more than a party. It is a religious ceremony. Having people break in at different points in the Seder, stay for a while, then leave for the Seder around the corner, destroyed its real meaning. That's when the Jewish custom of the afikoman began.

No one can leave the Seder until the afikoman has been shared. And no one can eat again that evening after the afikoman has been eaten. The Jews may lean at the table as the Romans did, but they could not accept Roman customs that harmed Judaism.

The afikoman rules made possible the custom of "stealing" the afikoman. The Seder cannot be completed until the afikoman has been eaten. No other piece of matzah will do. So the children "steal" it from where the father has set it aside. He has to "ransom" the afikoman from them before he can declare the Seder over. (Many a family has invented "hide the matzah" games to make the afikoman hunt much fun after dinner.)

Telling the Pesaḥ story

After the breaking of the matzah, the father begins the telling of the Pesaḥ story. This is the main purpose of the Seder and the Pesaḥ celebration. It starts with an announcement. The father uncovers the matzah and says: "This is the bread of slavery which our forefathers ate in Egypt when they were slaves. Let all who are hungry come and share this meal with us. Let all who are needy come now and celebrate the Pesaḥ with us."

In olden times the door was actually opened while this was said so any poor Jew could come and share the Seder. But this is not practical in large cities and in modern times. In any case, it is better to give a poor man enough so he can celebrate the Seder in his own home with his own family than have him come to another person's house. But we still recite the ancient invitation to remind us of our Jewish duties to the poor.

The youngest child now asks the Four Questions. Why is this important duty given the youngest child? Because the Festival of Freedom is as much for the

THE SEDER

Seder means "order." The Seder feast is a religious ceremony conducted by the father of the family. The wine and the special foods are symbols to remind us of our slavery in Egypt and our escape to freedom.

children as for the adults. Remember, the law says it is for parents to teach their children the story of their ancestors. They must know this story so that they will do all they can in their lives to make men more free and society more just.

The father begins to answer the questions and immediately starts telling new stories. One is about the four sons, one was wise, one stubborn, one simple, and one unknowing. One knows about Passover, one doesn't care, one would like to know, and the last one doesn't know anything special is going on. Still, we must tell the Pesaḥ story to all of them, to all types of children.

The story continues and the ten plagues with which God punished the Egyptians are recited. As each plague is pronounced, one drop of wine is spilled from each wineglass. Wine is the symbol of happiness; by spilling a drop with each plague we take away a little happiness. We do this because the plagues hurt and killed other human beings. This is no cause for happiness. Even if it is our enemies who are hurt, we must not rejoice.

A Midrash tells us that after the Jews got safely across the Sea of Reeds, and the sea closed, drowning the Egyptian army, the angels then wanted to sing praises to God at this sign of His power. But God stopped them. "How can you be happy," He asked, "when human beings, whom I created, are dying?" This is in keeping with the lesson in the Book of Proverbs that teaches "Do not rejoice when your enemy falls, and be not glad when he stumbles."

Next comes the list of miracles God performed for the Jews in bringing them out of Egypt. After every one we say *Dayenu*, "That alone would have been enough to do for us." And it is one of the many songs which are sung.

The commandment blessings

Then the second cup of wine is drunk. It is almost time for the meal, but first the Motzi must be said. And since it is a commandment to eat matzah this night we must also say the commandment blessing:

וְצִוָּנוּ עַל־אֲכִילַת מַצָּה:

and commanded us to eat matzah.

Then, after the commandment blessing for the bitter herbs:

וְצִוָּנוּ עַל־אֲכִילַת מָרוֹר

and commanded us to eat bitter herbs

we dip the bitter herbs in ḥaroset, and eat them. The bitter herbs—usually horseradish or plain radish—remind us of the bitterness of slavery. The ḥaroset, which looks like the cement the Jews had to make when they were building cities for Pharaoh, is sweet. Together, the maror and ḥaroset remind us that all life is a mixture of the bitter and the sweet.

And as another reminder of the ancient days, we eat maror and ḥaroset in a matzah sandwich as Hillel did.

The Passover feast

Then dinner is served. All the Jewish holidays have special meals. But the Passover feast is the greatest of them. Maybe it's because we're so hungry after the first part of the Seder. Maybe it's because we want to show we're free. But lots of things are served and everyone eats and eats. That too is part of the celebration.

The close of the Seder

After the meal, the father must find the afikoman, or "ransom" it from whoever has it. He shares it among all the guests and the dinner is over.

Grace after the meal is said and the third cup of wine is drunk. Then the door of the house is opened for the prophet Elijah.

AWAITING ELIJAH

Near the close of the Seder feast the door is opened for the prophet Elijah. According to tradition Elijah will come before the coming of the Messiah. By opening the door Jews show that they not only remember God's help in the past—they are looking forward to the Kingdom of God.

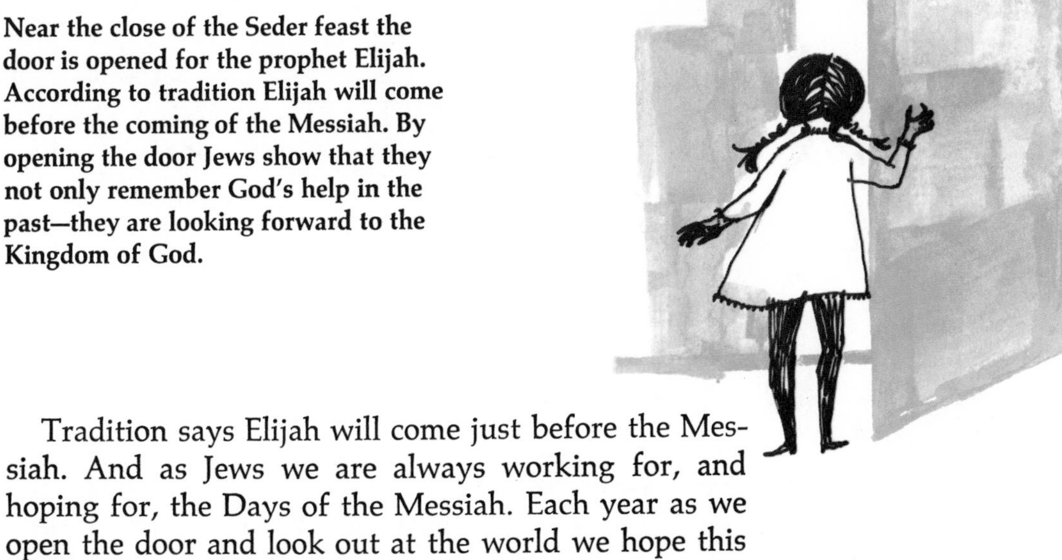

Tradition says Elijah will come just before the Messiah. And as Jews we are always working for, and hoping for, the Days of the Messiah. Each year as we open the door and look out at the world we hope this will be the time he comes and all men will be made happy. By such a simple thing as opening a door we do what our families have done for hundreds of years, what our people are doing Pesaḥ night everywhere, and what we Jews intend to keep doing till the Kingdom of God is on earth.

Then there are prayers, the fourth cup of wine, and some delightful songs to sing until very late.

The Seder is not the whole of Pesaḥ. It is only the beginning of the celebration of freedom and the spring. But the Seder sets the tone. All during the week that follows, whether we are at services or eating matzah with our lunch, we will remember. It is not so long ago that Jews were treated worse than slaves by the Nazis in Germany. And there are many people in the world today who are not much better off than slaves. But we are free. Pesaḥ is not just about the past. It is about today and tomorrow, about what Jews should be doing with their time all their lives.

12

Spring into summer: the Omer

Tying Pesaḥ to Shavuot

Every Jewish holiday is celebrated for several reasons; every Jewish holiday has several stories about its beginning. But of all the special days in the calendar the days of the *Omer*, and the holiday that comes near the middle of those days—Lag ba-Omer—has the oddest combination of reasons and backgrounds and stories.

עוֹמֶר

Most holidays are either joyous or sad; most holidays are mainly history or mainly nature; the Omer days are both very sad and very joyous, bound to nature and bound to history.

The Bible says that on the second day of Pesaḥ, we begin counting the days of the Omer. On the 50th day of the counting, the festival of Shavuot begins. So, in a way, the holidays of Pesaḥ and Shavuot are tied together by the days of the counting of the Omer, the *Sefirah* days. (Sefirah means "counting" in Hebrew.)

There's a reason for tying together two of the most important holidays in the Jewish calendar—Pesaḥ and

FROM PESAḤ TO SHAVUOT

The fifty days between Pesaḥ and Shavuot are called the days of the Counting of the Omer. In Temple times an omer (or sheaf) of barley was brought to the Temple each day and prayers and blessings were said.

Shavuot—through the Omer days. First, this tying together gives the season a rhythm—happy, sad, happy, sad, happy. But more important, this arrangement gives special importance to the meanings of the two big holidays.

Pesaḥ is the holiday of freedom. Shavuot is the holiday of the giving of the Torah. The days of the Omer are not really holidays at all—except for Lag ba-Omer, which is a kind of holiday. It's as if we were being told that you can't have feasts and celebrations every day; that life isn't all one big party.

Freedom isn't enough by itself. Freedom doesn't mean we have the right to do anything we wish. In freedom we can do foolish things, bad things, as well as good things. Tying Pesaḥ to Shavuot through the days of the Omer teaches us that the value of freedom depends on what we do with freedom, that freedom must be linked with law—God's law—which means linked with good. Freedom is best when it is used in God's service, in trying to make ourselves more like God.

For this, God sets us an example. God does not make puppets out of us, so we can do only that which is good. He gives us freedom. Nor does He take that freedom away even when we act foolishly. We should do good—but because we choose to, not because we have no other choice. And as God gives us freedom, so we must cherish this gift and try to spread it to all peoples.

Bringing the barley sheaves

Pesaḥ is celebrated when the first barley was harvested in ancient days in the Land of Israel. On the second day of Pesaḥ a bundle of the newly harvested barley was brought to the Temple as a sacrifice, as a gift to God. And every day thereafter, for 49 days, another sheaf of barley was brought to the Temple.

The ceremony when the priests received the sheaf of barley included blessings, prayers, and singing of psalms. In particular, Psalm 67 was recited because it says, "The earth has given her produce; may God, our God, bless us." And the priest would announce, "This is the first (or tenth, or thirtieth) day of the counting of the sheaves." (The Hebrew word for "sheaf" is *omer*.)

Although sheaves of barley are not brought to the synagogue today, the days of the Omer are counted at services each day between Pesaḥ and Shavuot.

In ancient times, and even today in places where men live by what they grow, the spring is a time of great worry. The food put aside from the autumn harvests is almost gone; perhaps it is all gone. Life depends on the new crops still in the ground. Life depends on the sun and the rain and the proper combination of both.

A time of waiting—and watching

In ancient Judea, the barley harvest had begun by Pesaḥ, but the rest of the food crops had not yet been harvested. (Shavuot celebrates the second harvest.) So, from Pesaḥ to Shavuot, the people watched the skies and the earth and prayed for good crops to feed them through the year.

During such unsure seasons, people did not make merry. They waited, and worried, and watched, and wondered. It was a time for hope—and for faith. So the days of the counting of the Omer were quiet days.

A TIME OF WATCHING AND WAITING

After the first barley harvest, at Pesaḥ, the Jews awaited the second harvest, at Shavuot, when other food crops would be ripe. The harvest, and the welfare of the community depended on rain. The ceremonies at the Temple as the barley sheaves were brought each day included prayers for rain. The counting of the Omer bound the Jews together during this time of waiting.

There was no dancing, no feasting, no celebrating. Much of the rest of the year would depend on its being a good spring.

That's the earliest reason we can think of for the counting of the Omer, and for the sadness of these days. In the old days, and even today among traditional Jews, there are no marriages during this time because marriages are joyful celebrations and include feasting. There are no fancy parties, no parading of new clothes, between Pesaḥ and Shavuot. In the old days Jews didn't even cut their hair during the regular Sefirah days, nor do Orthodox Jews today.

A legend of Rabbi Akiva

That's the nature reason for the days of Omer. But Lag ba-Omer, like other Jewish holidays, has other reasons behind it—historical reasons, religious reasons.

In the year 70 C.E. the Romans captured the city of Jerusalem and destroyed the Second Temple. After the first shock of the destruction had worn off, the Jews tried to rebuild, if not a state, at least a civilization of Jews. The Rabbis gathered at the village Yavneh to interpret the Law, as the high court—the Sanhedrin—had done before. Schools were opened and study continued. The synagogues became the center of religious life instead of the Temple.

At first, the Jews were successful in building a new life. But their success depended on who was emperor in Rome, and who was the emperor's governor over them. About 60 years after the fall of the Temple, the situation was desperate. The Romans threatened to build a pagan temple on the site where the Temple had stood. Under the leadership of Rabbi Akiva and of Bar Kokhba, the Jews revolted.

Rabbi Akiva was the greatest scholar of his time. He was said to have had thousands of students. In fact, every student in Judea said that he was a student of Rabbi Akiva. In the middle of the revolt, say our legends, during the months of Nisan and Iyar, during the Sefirah days, a terrible plague swept Palestine and thousands of Rabbi Akiva's students died. That tragedy made the ordinary sadness of the days of the Omer even greater.

ל״ג בָּעוֹמֶר

But on the eighteenth of Iyar, which is the thirty-third day of the counting of the Omer, the plague suddenly stopped. The rest of the students of Rabbi Akiva were saved. So that day, Lag ba-Omer (*lag, lamed-gimel,* is 33 in Hebrew) became a sort of holiday, the happy day of the saving of the students of the Law.

A legend of Simeon ben Yoḥai

Another great scholar during this time, Rabbi Simeon ben Yoḥai, is also part of the Lag ba-Omer legend. Despite the Roman law forbidding teaching of the Torah, Rabbi Simeon continued to meet his students and to explain the great Law of Moses. The Romans sent soldiers to find him and bring him to trial, but Rabbi Simeon and his son escaped. They found refuge in a cave in the Galilee hills. There they hid for 13 years, living on the fruit of the carob tree that grew outside the cave—and on water from a spring.

Once each year, the children of Galilee would risk the Romans to go to visit the hidden teacher—who was a criminal according to the Romans. The children could not go directly to the cave because the Romans might have followed them. Instead, they took what looked like picnic lunches and bows and arrows, and went into the woods dressed as hunters. They did this once each year, in the spring when it was possible to go into the hills. And every year it was on the same day—the eighteenth of Iyar, the thirty-third day of the counting of the Omer.

Lag ba-Omer, a spring holiday

A joyous occasion is celebrated with feasting and merrymaking. So Lag ba-Omer became a day on which celebrations were allowed. That's why, although custom says there should be no weddings during the Sefirah days, they are permitted on Lag ba-Omer.

LAG BA-OMER LEGENDS

According to Jewish customs there were to be no weddings or happy celebrations during the days of counting the Omer, the Sefirah days. But an exception is made for Lag ba-Omer, the 33rd day. That is a happy day, a holiday. On that day a plague once ceased and many students of Rabbi Akiva were spared from death by plague. And on that day, during the rebellion of Bar Kokhba, Jewish children went into woods to visit the scholar Simeon ben Yoḥai and his son who were hiding from the Romans.

And because Lag ba-Omer is connected with the histories of two great scholars, Rabbi Akiva and Rabbi Simeon ben Yoḥai, it became a spring holiday for Jewish schools in Eastern Europe. It has lately taken on a new meaning: Lag ba-Omer is also *Yom ha-Moreh*, the Day of the Teacher, when many American Jewish communities honor their teachers.

Lag ba-Omer is not widely celebrated because it is not a major holiday. Even the rules about sadness during the days of Omer are not widely followed because Conservative Jews have modified them and Reform Jews have given them up altogether.

Days of counting the Omer

Still the days of the counting of the Omer say many things to anyone who cares about the Jewish calendar.

They mark the natural disasters and the man-made disasters that befell the Jewish people.

They mark the worrisome days when people waited

A NEW HOLIDAY

New customs arise as Jewish history goes on. Now the 5th of Iyar may be celebrated as a happy holiday even though it comes in the Omer days. That is the day (in 1948) when Israel became a free and independent state.

through the early spring to find out whether they would have enough to eat that year.

They mark the sad story of the last great revolt of the Jews against the Romans.

They mark the dedication of our great scholars who insisted on teaching the Torah even at the risk of death.

But the days of Omer include happy days, too.

Lag ba-Omer marks the saving of the students from the plague.

It recalls the children going to the woods to visit Rabbi Simeon, carrying bows and arrows to fool the Romans.

It is today Scholars' Day and Teachers' Day.

And since 1948 the days of Omer include Israel Independence Day, the 5th of Iyar, and this day also is celebrated as a holiday.

It is an old, old custom to count the 50 days and many people do not even know about it. But it is another way that the Jewish people found to take each springtime and use it as a time for remembering who they are and what they are trying to do among men.

13

Summer: Shavuot

Why we need rules

If you were all alone on an island in the middle of the ocean, you wouldn't really need any rules to live by. You could do exactly as you wished when you wished—although even then you *should* follow the first four Commandments: the laws about God and the Sabbath. But as soon as one other person appeared, you would have to have some rules about what you should and shouldn't do. And the more people, the more rules.

Some rules would be to make things easy: Don't stick your hand in someone else's food dish; drive on the right side of the road. Some rules would try to make things fair: Don't come into my tent unless I give permission. And if there were a genius around, or a Prophet, the rules would also be a kind of dream of what men ought to be: Don't bear a grudge; love your neighbor.

With billions of people in the world, with millions

packed together in giant cities, rules are necessary and dreams important. We need rules to keep us from bumping into each other. But equally, we need rules that teach us decency and humanity; rules that protect the weak and the young; rules that give everyone a chance to grow up and be a good person.

Luckily, every new generation does not have to draw up a completely new set of rules. The young often feel like tearing up all the old rules and creating new ones. But if they did—and some generations have tried it—the new rules would be very much like the old.

Right and wrong

The way in which we understand and follow rules is an important measure of our growing up.

A baby follows no rules at all. It yells when it wants attention. It doesn't care what time it is or whatever else is happening. A young child has to be told repeatedly what is the proper—the right—thing to do. From this repetition, and from the example of older people, he learns rules and habits of doing good.

A grown person knows many rules for living. He tries to apply the right one to each new situation. That is not always easy. It helps to remember the difference between the rules that make life pleasant and the rules that make life important. For example, there's the rule that you shouldn't eat mashed potatoes with your fingers. This rule should be followed to get along with

THE GIVING OF THE TORAH

Men need rules and laws to guide them in being just and fair to each other. The greatest rules are the laws given in the Torah. Shavuot celebrates God's giving the Torah to the Jewish people.

people in our society. But that rule is a lot less important than the rule that you shouldn't pick on little kids. That not only makes them unhappy and denies them justice, but it will, in time, turn you into a bully. That sort of rule is about people and doing good. We call that ethics. The rules of ethics are the most important kind of rules in Judaism.

The Jewish religion has taught that what a person does is far more important than what he believes. This is particularly true of what he does to and with other people. So the Jews developed very many, sometimes very complicated, rules for living with other people. They have passed on these laws from generation to generation for 3,500 years.

The giving of the Torah

The heart of the Jews' rules for living is the Torah. At Mount Sinai, where the Jews of Moses' time were given the Torah, they pledged to follow God's rules. To this day, we believe that by following these rules we serve God. Not only as individuals but also as a people, by what we do together in our communities. We want to set an example to all the peoples of the world, so they, too, will come to follow these holy rules of conduct.

Shavuot is the holiday on which we celebrate God's giving to us the Torah. We call this holiday the "Time of the Giving of the Torah." Not the "receiving" of the Torah but the "giving" of the Torah. A Ḥasidic Rabbi gave two reasons why:

First, we were *given* the Torah only once, in Moses' time, on Shavuot, but every Jew in every generation *receives* the Torah whenever he studies.

Second, while every Jew is *given* the Torah equally, not every Jew *receives* it equally. Some Jews understand it better than others; some Jews follow it more closely than others.

So we celebrate its giving, not its receiving.

THE PEOPLE'S BIRTHDAY

Shavuot, the Festival of the First Fruits and the holiday celebrating the giving of the Torah, is a kind of birthday for the Jewish people. In accepting the Torah at Mount Sinai, 3,200 years ago, they took on the special way of life that made them Jews.

A harvest festival

That is one reason for Shavuot, but like all Jewish festivals, there is also a reason in nature. Shavuot is called in the Torah, *Ḥag ha-Katzir*, the Festival of the Grain Harvest. And it is *Ḥag ha-Bikkurim*, the Festival of the First Fruits. On Shavuot we celebrate the fulfillment of the promise of spring.

Shavuot means "weeks." It is celebrated seven weeks after Pesaḥ. Pesaḥ marks the beginning of the barley harvest. For seven weeks, through the days of the counting of the Omer, the barley harvest was completed and the wheat harvest begun. That harvest period ended with the Feast of (the Seven) Weeks—Shavuot. It's the story of spring turning into summer, of freedom ripening through law. On Shavuot, two loaves of bread, made from the newly harvested wheat, were brought to the Temple and offered as a gift to God.

It is a lovely season. The spring rains are over and the land is heavy with green. The heat of summer has not yet begun. Not only the grain had ripened in the Land of Israel: the grapes had turned purple; the first honey had been taken from the hive; other fruits were full and ready for plucking. These, too, were to be shared with God on Shavuot.

PARTNERS WITH GOD

In Temple times, Jews brought the first fruits of the season to the Temple as an offering to God. They shared with Him, as partners, because together He and they had made the harvest possible. And by remembering and obeying the Torah Jews share with God as partners in bringing the Torah to life.

That the Jews shared things with God is one of the most important ideas of Shavuot. The Jews brought their first fruits to the Temple to give to God, not to pay their landlord, not because they had to. They came to share their first fruits with God as one partner shares with another.

In partnership, God and man make the earth live. God provides sun and rain and warmth. Man provides seed and skill and labor. Together, God and man produce the fruits of the earth. On Shavuot, man shares with God the produce of their joint work—and he remembers what he and God are trying to do for all men, everywhere.

Shavuot in the Temple

Naturally, harvest time is a time of happiness and rejoicing. In ancient days the farmers brought their first fruits to the Temple as a small gift to God in thanks for His great gifts. The Mishnah tells us about it:

All the farmers from the countryside would gather outside the walls of the nearest city. They formed a procession led by an ox whose horns had been decorated with gold and with olive branches. Each man carried a gaily decorated basket filled with his first fruits. If the city was near Jerusalem, they carried ripe figs and grapes; if the city was far from Jerusalem (and the fresh fruits might spoil on the way) they carried dried fruits and raisins.

At the gates of Jerusalem they were met by the people of the city, who said: "Enter in peace our brothers from . . . [Dan, or Galilee, or wherever they came from]."

Still led by musicians playing their instruments, the procession climbed the hill to the Temple. They entered the courtyard of the Temple where they were met by a chorus of Levites. Holding his basket of fruits on his shoulder, each man said: "This day have I given unto the Lord." He then handed his basket to a priest who blessed it and placed it before the altar.

A changing holiday

That's how the main Shavuot celebration went in the days of the Temple. But when the Temple was destroyed in the year 70, the holiday had to change. Many Jews were no longer farmers. Many lived in lands in which the harvest times were different. In northern climates, wheat was not ready for harvest at Shavuot, nor were the grapes ripe.

That's probably why what was mostly the holiday of the first fruits became mostly the holiday of the giving of the Torah.

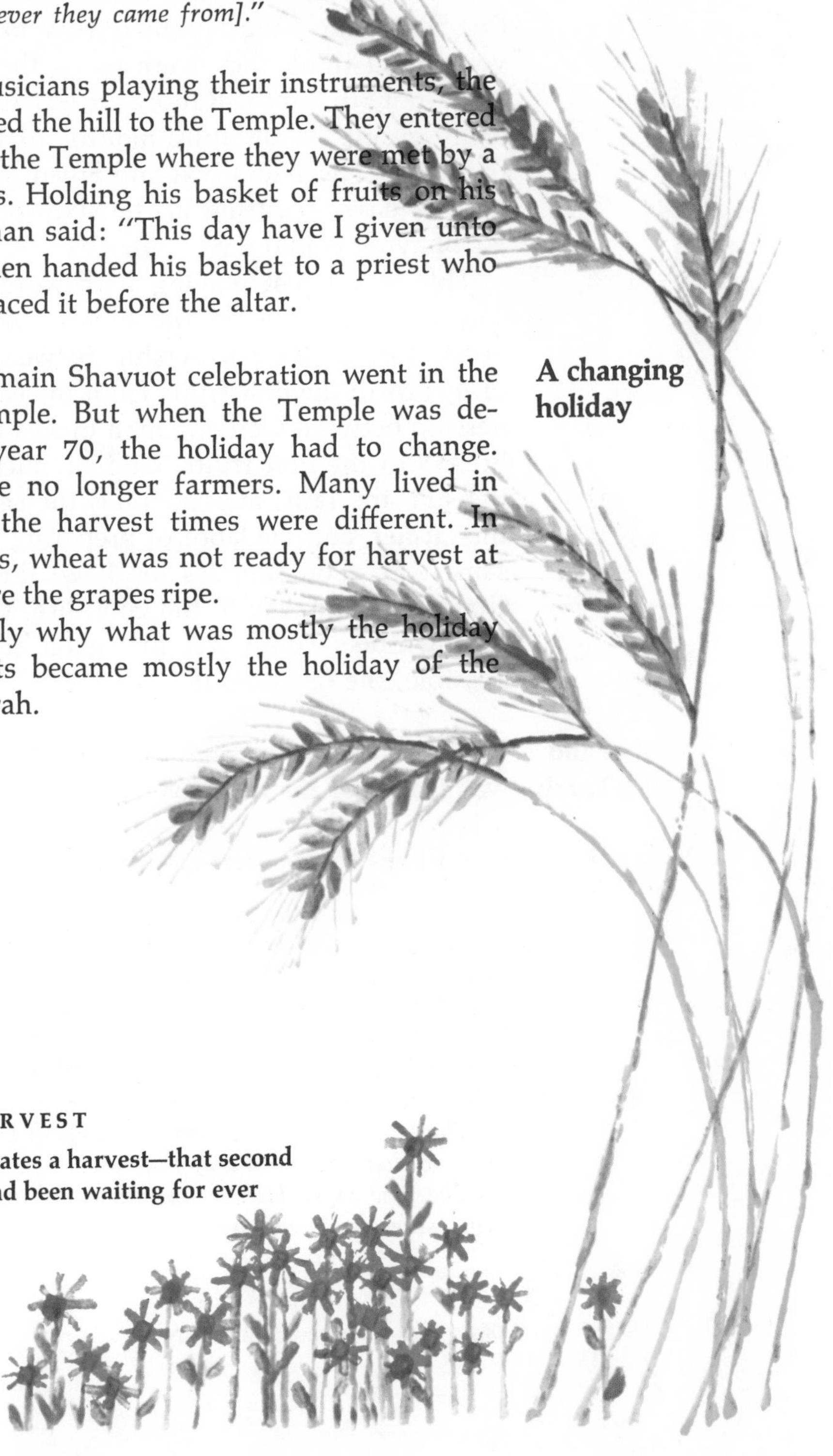

A SECOND HARVEST

Shavuot also celebrates a harvest—that second harvest the Jews had been waiting for ever since Pesaḥ.

The Bible says that the Children of Israel reached Mount Sinai three months after they left Egypt. If the first Seder marks the day the Jews went out from Egypt, you would think they were given the Torah 90 days later—not 50. But the Rabbis ruled that "three months" really meant "in the third month" of their leaving. So there were Nisan and Iyar and Sivan. And if you figure out the days, counting in the sixth of Sivan, you get 50. Shavuot is that day.

This is not just playing with words and numbers. The two meanings of the holiday are close to each other. Just as the partnership between man and God brings forth the first fruits from the earth, so the partnership between God and man makes the Law come to life. With the first fruits, God supplies the rich earth, the sun, the rain; man supplies the seed, the skills of the farmer, and the labor of preparing the earth. In the same way, God supplies the Law; the Jews accept it. God points the way to the good life; the Jews, by following God's Torah, live that good life. God makes it possible; the Jew does it.

Man and the Torah

That's another thing Shavuot reminds us of: The Torah was made for man. It was not made to be worshiped; it is not an idol. It was given to man for his everyday use. Rabbi Joshua ben Levi told a story about this:

When Moses went up to receive the Torah, the angels objected. "What is a man doing up here?" they cried. "Do You propose to give this Torah to someone of flesh and blood?"

God told Moses to answer the angels. Moses said, "What is written in this Law? 'I am the Lord your God who brought you forth from Egypt.' Were you angels enslaved by Pharaoh? What need do you have of the Torah?

"The Law says, 'Remember the Sabbath Day.' Do the angels work so that they need a day of rest?

"The Law says, 'Honor thy father and thy mother.' Do you have fathers and mothers?

"It says 'do not steal, do not murder, do not covet.' You angels are never tempted to do such things."

Then the angels praised God who had made the Torah for man and were happy that Moses had come to get it.

Putting the Torah holiday together with the harvest holiday is also a good idea because the holiday of the harvest is a holiday for all men, not only for Jews. All who plow the earth and care for the young shoots, who yearn for the rain to water their crops, share in the gifts we celebrate on Shavuot. And all men who desire it may share in the Torah that was given to us on Mount Sinai; all men can, if they will, follow those rules and guidelines to the good life.

The Rabbis often said: The Torah is open to everyone. It was given openly, in the desert, amid fire and water. The Bible makes a point of the fire and water and desert because each of these is important to life and each is free to everyone. So, too, the words of the Law are necessary to all and free to all.

Here is another explanation: If the Torah had been given in the Land of Israel, the other nations could have said, "We can't share it." Instead, the Torah was given in a place that had no owners, in the desert.

That's how Shavuot became the holiday of the giving of the Torah—or the sharing of the Torah. And since the Children of Israel, the descendants of Abraham, Isaac, and Jacob, became a holy nation on that day, Shavuot is really the birthday of the Jews.

Shavuot was originally a one-day festival. In Orthodox and Conservative synagogues it is observed a second day.

Shavuot in the synagogue

The holiday is marked by special services in the synagogue, by decorations special to the season, and like many Jewish holidays, by special foods.

It has long been a custom to decorate the synagogue

with branches and leaves and with the first fruits of the trees and the vines. The pious people would make it a point to stay up all night reading a collection of pieces from the Jews' greatest books. It was a nice way of saying one was pleased to have the Torah.

In the morning service many beautiful poems were sung in honor of the holiday. But the most important part comes when the Torah is read. On Shavuot we always read the Ten Commandments.

Another interesting part of the service is the reading of the Book of Ruth. It is a fitting story for this holiday for two reasons. First, a big part of the book takes place in the fields during the barley harvest. Second, Ruth tells the story of the Moabite girl who is accepted by the Jews as a Jew. This young girl, born a worshiper of idols, accepts God and the Torah. King David was her great grandson! And since the Messiah is supposed to come from the family of David, he too will have in his family someone who was born an idol worshiper.

The lesson of Ruth—and of Shavuot—is that birth and family are not of primary importance; what is most important is how you live. A good and holy person lives by a set of rules that divides good from evil. For Jews, this set of rules is the Torah.

Shavuot today

Today, the celebration of Shavuot is very much as it was during our great-grandfathers' day. The synagogue is decorated with green shoots and first fruits. The Ten Commandments and Ruth are still read as part of the service. The one great change in the celebration of Shavuot is an addition. Many synagogues today hold their Confirmation ceremonies on or near Shavuot. For too many young Jews, Jewish education stops when they reach age 13, with Bar or Bat Mitzvah. But at that age they have only begun to learn what a Jew is and how to be a Jew. So many synagogues continue Jewish

SHAVUOT IN THE SYNAGOGUE

The synagogue is decorated with first fruits for Shavuot. The Ten Commandments are read during the service, and the story of Ruth is read. Ruth is a harvest story that shows that what is important about a person is not his birth or family but that he accepts and obeys the Torah.

education for at least two more years—ending with a kind of graduation called *Confirmation*.

And since all Jewish education is based on Torah, what better day to celebrate that than on the day the Torah was given to the Jews? So, on that day, at Confirmation, each young person accepts the Torah personally. He makes it his or her guide for life.

Shavuot reminds us that life should be a partnership between each person and God. Together we can create good things like growing food. Together we can create good people and a good society. That is what our time is given to us for, spring and summer, fall and winter, year after year.

14

Fall: Sukkot

Living and working

To live is to work. For animals of every kind, from ants to elephants, life is the endless work of searching for food. And although man has invented many marvelous machines we still must work. There are a few very rich people who neither have to work or try to work. But they keep on searching for new pleasures—and that becomes their work.

There is joy in work although most of us complain about having to do it. One of the greatest pleasures we have is to do a job and know we did it well.

Jews have always thought work was important. And doing your work well was even more important. Jews believe that the world can be made better—and the way to make it better is to work hard for a better world. Jews remember that their history was full of struggle—which is a form of work. Life was hard during the 40 years in which the Jews wandered in the wilderness.

They lived through this time and reached the Promised Land. One reason was that they didn't quit because things were hard. Another was that they had God's help. So they rejoiced when they got to the Land of Israel.

To this day we rejoice each year at the end of the year's work—and the beginning of the next year's work. Soon after our Jewish New Year comes one of the happiest of our holidays, the Festival of Sukkot. As Pesaḥ comes with the hope of spring and Shavuot celebrates the new summer, so Sukkot is our time to celebrate the fall season and all that the past months have brought us.

Harvest time

In ancient days, farmers lived in villages for protection and company. Every morning they went out to their fields and every evening they came home to their village.

But when the grapes were ripe and the wheat was heavy on the stalk, there was no time to go back and forth. The harvest could not wait. The grapes might start turning or a sudden storm might beat the heavy wheat to the ground. The harvesters worked from first light to first star. So they built little huts in the field in which to live during the harvesting. (Some Bedouin still do this today.)

These huts were called *sukkot*.

The harvest was a time of great thanksgiving. It was the time when man reaped the good things that his labor had produced. It was a time of feasting and giving joyful thanks to God for the food that had grown out of the earth, for that food meant life.

So the time of the harvest, when the people lived in sukkot, became a holiday that was also called Sukkot.

It was a holiday of nature much like Pesaḥ. Like Pesaḥ, it was celebrated at the full moon. Like Pesaḥ, it lasted a full week. And just as Pesaḥ welcomes the season of spring dew in the Land of Israel, so Sukkot marks the beginning of fall rains.

Remembering a journey

But for the Jew the holiday must have historical meaning, too. Pesaḥ celebrates the Exodus; Shavuot the giving of the Torah. Sukkot continues the story. It marks the 40-year journey in the wilderness. For during that journey, tradition says, our ancestors escaped the sun by living in huts, or sukkot. These huts were put up as temporary shelters during their wandering. With God's help they survived. They did come to the Holy Land and permanent homes.

Now, as each generation of Jews builds its sukkot, it remembers the hard journey the Jews once made and the help God gave them on the way. And we celebrate the help He gives us on our hard way.

Sukkot, God's festival

During ancient Bible days, before the Jews were taken in exile to Babylon, this holiday was called *Ḥag ha-Asif*, the Festival of the Harvest. And because it was a very joyous time, it was also called *Zeman Simḥatenu*, the happy season. It was probably during the Babylonian Exile, when the building of the sukkah became the main symbol of the holiday, that it got the name *Sukkot*.

Sukkot was the main holiday of the Jews in Bible times since most of them were farmers and their whole lives depended on the harvest. Once the main harvest was in, they could stop to enjoy themselves. They called it *he-Ḥag*, The Festival, as if it were the best or most important one. The Bible used another name that shows how important it was—*Ḥag Adonai*, God's Festival.

According to the Torah, every man was supposed to go up to Jerusalem for Pesaḥ, Shavuot, and Sukkot. But the average farmer could not leave his fields during the spring planting. Nor could he go to Jerusalem during the middle of the growing season on Shavuot. But by Sukkot the last harvest was in. The main work was completed for the year. He could take some time off to go to Jerusalem. So many went and Sukkot became the most popular festival.

The commandment to go to Jerusalem was for all Jews everywhere. However, travel was slow and dangerous. It took at least two weeks to come from Babylon and then you had to wait for a big caravan to form so there was protection from robbers. It took much longer for the Jews of Greece and Rome and Egypt and Spain to get to Jerusalem. Therefore they could not come often. But when they did come it was usually for Sukkot.

Building the sukkah

Of all the festivals, Sukkot has had to change most because we live so differently today than we used to. Pesaḥ is much as it was a thousand years ago. We can avoid ḥametz and eat matzah and have our Seder just as our ancestors did. On Shavuot we still read the Ten

THE FALL HARVEST FESTIVAL

Sukkot has been called the Harvest Festival or the Happy Season, God's Festival, or just the Festival.

BUILDING THE SUKKAH

God commanded each family to build a sukkah in memory of the huts the Jews had in the wilderness. (Harvesters also lived in huts.)

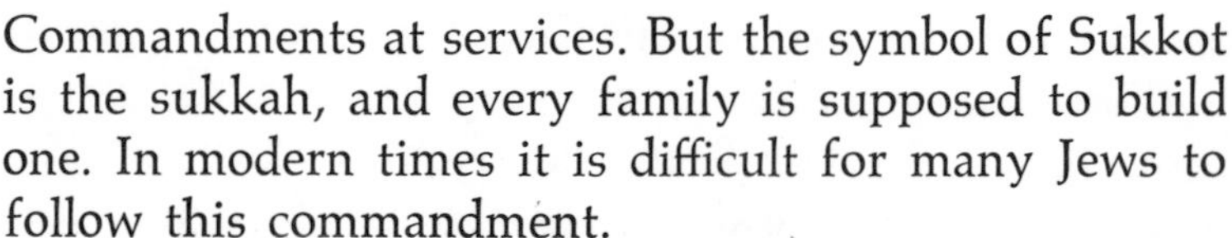

Commandments at services. But the symbol of Sukkot is the sukkah, and every family is supposed to build one. In modern times it is difficult for many Jews to follow this commandment.

The Rabbis laid down specifications concerning the building of the sukkah. It must be no higher than 30 feet. It must have at least three walls. The roof must be of leaves and straw, with enough open space so that the stars can be seen through the roof.

Building a sukkah has become a synagogue practice for many people rather than an individual family one. Every synagogue sets up a sukkah. Usually it is big and beautiful, with many kinds of fruits and vegetables as decorations. As part of the Sukkot celebration in the synagogue, everyone goes into the sukkah. Kiddush is made there. Traditional Jews eat their meals in the sukkah, and some people sleep there as well.

לוּלָב

Harvest symbols

אֶתְרוֹג

A harvest festival needs symbols of the good things harvested. So the other Sukkot symbols are the Lulav and Etrog. The *Etrog* is the fruit of the citron tree, a beautiful lemonlike fruit. The Bible calls it the "fruit of a goodly tree." The Bible also tells us to take "branches of palm trees, of leafy trees, and of the willow of the brook." *Lulav* really means "palm branch," but we give that name to all three branches when they are put together. It is made of a small holder with the palm branch in the middle and with the thick boughs of a sweet-smelling myrtle tree and the willows of the brook on either side of it.

The Lulav and Etrog were carried on Sukkot as symbols of the harvest. They still are. But over the years, many Rabbis have found religious meaning in the Lulav and Etrog.

Meaning of Lulav and Etrog

According to one explanation, the Lulav and Etrog stand for the main parts of the body. The Etrog is the heart, the palm is the spine, the myrtle is the eye, and the willow is the mouth. Put them all together and they praise God for the good harvest. So a good man will not just be religious with his words or his feelings but he will try to serve God with all of him all the time.

A Midrash says that the four species of growing things stand for the Jewish people. Just as the Etrog has taste and fragrance, so some Jews have knowledge of the Torah and do good deeds. Just as the fruit of the palm (dates) has taste but no fragrance, so some Jews have knowledge of the Torah but do not do good deeds. Just as the myrtle has fragrance, but no taste, so some Jews have no knowledge of the Torah but do good deeds. And just as the willow has neither taste nor fragrance, so some Jews have no knowledge of the Torah and do not do good deeds.

But we tie them all together in the Lulav, and join them with the Etrog. So all Jews must stand together. The good Jews and the not-so-good Jews, the Orthodox, the Conservative, and the Reform Jews, and the Jews outside the synagogue, all are tied together as part of the Jewish people. When they stand together they are carrying out one of the oldest and most important parts of the Jewish tradition.

Another explanation of the Lulav and Etrog symbols is that the ancient Hebrews used them as a silent prayer for rain. When the priests marched around the altar holding the four species up to God, they were praying for rain. Just as these growing things could not have survived without rain, so we Jews cannot survive if the autumn rains do not come.

The Lulav and the Etrog mean these things and many more—good symbols always mean more than we can explain. When we hold the Lulav and Etrog we feel something that ties us to all other Jews in the world and to all the generations of Jews reaching back three thousand years—and to all the Jews that will yet be. And with them all we feel close to God.

Myrtle and willow do grow in many places where Jews live, but palm and citron do not. So they generally were—and still are—imported from the Land of Israel. This made them cost a great deal—far more than many families in Eastern Europe could afford in our grandparents' and great-grandparents' time. So families would get together to buy one Lulav and Etrog. A boy would be appointed guardian of the Lulav and Etrog and he would carry them from house to house every morning during Sukkot so each family could recite the special commandment blessing:

וְצִוָּנוּ עַל־נְטִילַת לוּלָב:

and commanded us to hold a Lulav [and Etrog].

Closing of Sukkot

According to the Bible, Sukkot was celebrated for seven days by the Jews of ancient Palestine. But it was followed immediately by a special closing holiday called *Atzeret*, "assembly." Sukkot was therefore really an eight-day festival, with the eighth day called *Atzeret*, or *Shemini Atzeret*, "the Eighth Day of Assembly."

When all the holidays got an extra day, an extra day was added to Atzeret so that Sukkot plus Atzeret lasted nine days. That ninth day came to be the holiday of Simḥat Torah. These two days are combined into one by Israeli as well as by Reform Jews.

The Lulav and Etrog are part of a beautiful ceremony during the morning service. As one of the special prayers is said, the worshiper points his Lulav and Etrog slowly in all four directions and up and down. By this, he shows that God is everywhere. In traditional synagogues the Lulav and Etrog are also paraded around while the congregation recites poems in praise of God and His works.

All during Sukkot (except Shabbat) the Lulav and Etrog are paraded once around the Bimah. On the seventh day the congregation parades around the Bimah seven times with their Lulav and Etrog. There are many

HARVEST SYMBOLS

The Lulav (palm, willow and myrtle) and Etrog (citron) are symbols of the harvest used in the ceremonies of Sukkot.

shouts of *Hoshana,* "God, help us," for that is an important part of the prayers. And because there are so many calls of *Hoshana,* people say that is why the seventh day has the special name *Hoshana Rabbah*—the Great Hoshana.

On the eighth day of Sukkot, on Shemini Atzeret, there are no Lulav and Etrog in the synagogue. It is not necessary to eat in the sukkah—although some people do. It is the closing of the great holiday of joy, an easing off. During the morning service of Shemini Atzeret the memorial services for the dead—Yizkor—are said.

And the congregation repeats a ceremony that goes back to the earliest days of the Jews—so far back that we have forgotten the beginnings of this ceremony.

This is the prayer for rain—*geshem*—the rain that will bring good crops if it comes in proper amount; the rain that will cause floods if it comes too heavily, or hunger if it does not come at all. The spring crops were watered by the spring dew and light rain. The summer was completely dry. That made the autumn rains especially important. They prepared the earth for the early winter and spring planting. This is true in Israel today even though there is much irrigation.

All Jews everywhere continue to pray for rain on Sukkot although they may live in a place where there is much water. But that doesn't mean that the prayers are empty. We pray for rain because we need it here, too. We also pray for rain because we care about our brother Jews in Israel. And we do so because rain is a symbol of God's mercy. He sends the rain on the rich and poor alike, on the good people and the bad, on the pious and the sinners. We pray that His rain, His mercy, will continue to fall upon the world and its people.

In the time of the Temple this prayer for rain had

many special ceremonies. Some *kibbutzim* (communal settlements) in Israel have created such ceremonies for themselves. At these kibbutzim the people gather at sunset on Shemini Atzeret on a hill where a brook begins. The children carry palm leaves and jugs. The adults carry torches and candles. A fire is built nearby. The children fill their jugs. They sing a song to the Bible verse:

> וּשְׁאַבְתֶּם־מַיִם בְּשָׂשׂוֹן מִמַּעַיְנֵי הַיְשׁוּעָה:
>
> *You shall draw water with gladness out of the springs of salvation.*

Then they pour the water over the fire—symbol of the ending of summer with the fall rain.

A holiday of faith

Sukkot does not celebrate what was, but what will be in nature and in history. It celebrates the fall harvest that *will feed* the people, not that *has fed* the people. It celebrates the autumn rain that has not yet fallen. Historically, it does not celebrate the entrance into the Promised Land, but the faith of our ancestors—in the middle of the wilderness—that they would find a home.

We may not really feel what it was like to live in huts as our ancestors did. But we can feel their faith and hope. Jews to this day manage to live through the most horrible times because they know that man and his world can become better—and will become better. How soon they become better depends partly on us. We are partners with God in creating that world.

In the Bible we are commanded to be joyful during Sukkot. That's odd, in a way. Commandments generally tell us what to do and what not to do: We must honor (obey and take care of) our parents; we must not steal or lie; we must feed the hungry, and so on. But the commandment for Sukkot tells us how we must *feel*. It's as if we were being shown that religion,

HOPE AND FAITH

The Bible commands that the Jews be joyful at Sukkot in celebrating the harvest that will feed the people and the rain that is still to fall. Then they remember and renew the faith and hope their ancestors showed in the wilderness before they came into the Promised Land.

and practices of religion, are not all solemn and dignified and grim. There is great joy in religion, great happiness in following the Law. Every season comes with its own message and its own joy. So year after year, Pesaḥ, Shavuot, and Sukkot, again and again, we are taught the happiness of making our time a good time by serving God.

15

The cycle ends: Simḥat Torah

Reading the Torah

Thanksgiving Day is about 300 years old. The Fourth of July is about 200 years old. Memorial Day is less than 100 years old. And Labor Day is about 50 years old. Simḥat Torah is more than a thousand years old, and Jews consider it a sort of new holiday. Simḥat Torah is really the second day of Shemini Atzeret. But it didn't become the Simḥat Torah we know until about the eleventh century.

Every Monday, Thursday, and Shabbat, a portion of the Torah is read in the synagogue. In the old days the portions read were rather small and so the entire Torah was read in three years. Then, in Babylonia, it became the custom to read longer portions. As a result, the entire Torah could be read through every year—and so a holiday was born. The reading of the Scroll is started on Simḥat Torah, and a year later, on Simḥat Torah, we reach the end. The last chapter of the last book of the Torah—Deuteronomy—is read. And immediately, we begin reading from the first chapter of the first book—Genesis. That is the chief ceremony of the day.

Because on this day we will complete reading the Torah and begin reading the Torah, we make it a holiday for rejoicing over the Torah.

The happiest holiday

Jews have many happy holidays, but the eve of Simḥat Torah is, traditionally, the happiest of them all. On this night our grandfathers sang and danced and ate and drank and cried with joy. They paraded with the Torah Scrolls in the synagogue. Sometimes they got so excited they danced in the synagogue and they danced in the streets outside the synagogue and they shouted

EVE OF SIMḤAT TORAH

Simḥat Torah eve is the happiest time of all. In our grandfathers' day, men danced with joy in the synagogue and in the streets, shouting and praising God. On that night only, in traditional synagogues, women and girls could come to the floor of the synagogue instead of staying in the balconies. Simḥat Torah is a day of rejoicing in Torah, the book of God's law. On that day the last chapters of the Torah are read, completing the year's reading. And on that day the first chapters are also read, beginning the new reading of the Book.

praises of God and His Torah. It was almost as if they were drunk with happiness over the Torah.

Most of us today are too shy to show our happiness so publicly. But there are communities of Ḥasidim in the United States and Israel where the same joyful sights can be seen on Simḥat Torah. And in the Soviet Union, where open celebrations of God and Torah can be dangerous, Jews who may never have read a Torah crowd outside the few synagogues and sing and dance in the streets to show that they remember.

Rejoicing in the synagogue

Traditional Jewish law allows only men on the floor of the synagogue. Women and girls sit in balconies, away from their husbands and fathers. But on the eve of Simḥat Torah the girls and women are allowed on the floor of the synagogue. That's how special a night it is.

One thing, very different, always happens on the eve of Simḥat Torah. It is the *Hakkafot*—the parades around the entire synagogue with the Torah. All the Torah Scrolls are taken out of the Ark; men and boys carry the Torah Scrolls up and down the aisles of the synagogue while the congregation chants special prayers and hymns. Many people will reach out to touch or kiss the Scrolls as they are carried past them. Every man and boy past Bar Mitzvah is given a chance to carry a Scroll during one of the Hakkafot. And the younger children march behind the older men carrying flags. Throughout the evening there is singing and afterward, naturally, something sweet to eat.

On the morning of Simḥat Torah comes the reading of the closing and opening chapters of the Torah. It is a special honor to be called to the Torah on the holiday when we are so joyous about the Torah. The man who recites the blessing over the last verse of Deuteronomy is called the *Ḥatan Torah,* the "bridegroom of the

REJOICING OF THE LAW

On Simḥat Torah, great Hakkafot, or parades, are held in the synagogue. Every man and boy of Bar Mitzvah age may carry a Scroll leading the parade. Smaller children carry flags.

Torah." The man who recites the blessing over the first chapter of Genesis is called the *Ḥatan Bereshit*, "the bridegroom of the beginning." The name "bridegroom" may sound strange, but in a way Jews are married to the Torah. And Simḥat Torah is supposed to be as happy as a wedding!

No one likes to be left out when we are celebrating on Simḥat Torah. So in many synagogues, after the Torah reading, all the small boys who have not yet become Bar Mitzvah are called up to the *Bimah*. They stand behind the reading desk, and a large Tallit is often held over their heads. An adult slowly recites the blessing over the Torah, a word or two at a time:

בָּרְכוּ אֶת־יְיָ הַמְבֹרָךְ:
בָּרוּךְ יְיָ הַמְבֹרָךְ לְעוֹלָם וָעֶד:
בָּרוּךְ אַתָּה יְיָ. אֱלֹהֵינוּ מֶלֶךְ הָעוֹלָם. אֲשֶׁר בָּחַר־בָּנוּ מִכָּל־
הָעַמִּים. וְנָתַן־לָנוּ אֶת־תּוֹרָתוֹ. בָּרוּךְ אַתָּה יְיָ. נוֹתֵן הַתּוֹרָה:

Bless the Lord, the blessed One.
Bless the Lord, who is blessed forever and ever.
Blessed art Thou, Lord our God, King of the universe, who has chosen us from among all peoples and has given us His Torah. Blessed art Thou, O Lord, giver of the Torah.

The young children repeat the words after him, thus sharing in the blessing. After concluding the Torah reading, the following blessing is recited:

בָּרוּךְ אַתָּה יְיָ. אֱלֹהֵינוּ מֶלֶךְ הָעוֹלָם. אֲשֶׁר נָתַן־לָנוּ תּוֹרַת
אֱמֶת. וְחַיֵּי עוֹלָם נָטַע בְּתוֹכֵנוּ. בָּרוּךְ אַתָּה יְיָ. נוֹתֵן הַתּוֹרָה:

Blessed art Thou, Lord our God, King of the universe, who has given us the Torah of truth and has implanted in us eternal life. Blessed art Thou, O Lord, giver of the Torah.

In this way the entire congregation of Jews shares in the "rejoicing of the Torah." The men and older boys, the women and girls, the youngest children. It is a day of the greatest joy for everyone, a day of feasting and dancing and singing. What is this Jewish feasting and dancing about? Not to celebrate a victory over another nation. Not to mark the birth or reign of a king. Not because the army is so strong or the hunters have killed many animals. This celebration is over a book, that is, the five books that make up the Torah.

THE BIGGEST JOB OF ALL

Jews rejoice in the Torah because it is the great guide in traveling the hardest, the most worthwhile road in life—the way of a good and upright person. On Simḥat Torah morning, great honor falls on the "bridegroom of the Torah," the man who is called to the Bimah to read the last chapter of Deuteronomy—and on the "bridegroom of the beginning," who is called to read the first chapter of Genesis. The day is happy like a wedding. The Jews are again "married" to the Law. Everyone must share in the joy, so even boys who are too young to have become Bar Mitzvah are called to the Bimah for a special blessing.

Among all the holidays of all the peoples of the world, this is perhaps the only holiday of great joy that celebrates a book. That says something special about our people. It tells us each year how we can learn to use our time well.

Joy in the Torah

It is hard to do difficult jobs well. It is hard to build a strong and beautiful house. It is hard to cure a stubborn illness. It is hard to get good marks in school. It is hard to go to Hebrew school and do additional studying when other children do not. So when we have done any of these things, and done them well, we are glad—we rejoice.

But harder than any of these tasks is to become a good and upright person. That's why we take great joy in the people that help us become good. We enjoy—and love—our parents, sisters and brothers, teachers, counselors, leaders who have helped us grow straight. Their help is a gift, and one way to repay them is to do as much for others.

But the greatest help for a Jew in becoming—and remaining—a good person is the Torah. This Book and the books that have grown out of it have guided Jews for several thousand years in their attempts to do good, be good, and build a good world. It would have been impossible to get as far in history as we have without the help of this Book.

No matter how bright we are, the Torah knows more than we do. No matter how much we know, we can learn more from the Torah. That's why we celebrate the fact that our people have devoted themselves to study of this Book for so many centuries and have passed it on to us. As we will pass it on to the generations that come after us.

The holiday of rejoicing in this Book, in the study of Torah, is Simḥat Torah.

Treasures of the Torah

A ship was leaving port for a distant city. The ship was filled with merchants and the goods they were taking to trade. Among the passengers was one scholar.

"What merchandise do you carry?" the merchants asked the scholar.

"The best," he answered. The merchants searched the ship to see what his merchandise was. They found nothing, only their own packages. So they laughed at him.

Midway across the sea a great storm arose and the ship was driven on the rocks. All the ship's cargo was lost but the passengers were saved. Eventually, all the passengers reached the city to which they were bound. The merchants had to beg for places to live and for food to eat. The scholar went to the synagogue of the city and asked for permission to deliver a lecture. His lecture showed that he was a great scholar, and he was asked to teach at the local academy. When the time came for him to go home, the leading members of the community gave him rich presents and came to the pier to say good-by.

The merchants who had been his shipmates were amazed. Then they asked the scholar to see if he could help them get home. Because he asked, the community paid their way home too.

Then they said, "You were right, Rabbi. Yours is the best merchandise."

That is the way the Jewish seasons come and go.

They begin each year with the spring; and each spring is celebrated with Passover, the holiday of freedom.

They continue each year into the summer; and each summer is celebrated by Shavuot, the holiday of the giving of the Law.

As the autumn follows the summer each year, so each year we celebrate Sukkot, the holiday of God's care and protection.

Then there is another ending and another beginning on Simḥat Torah. Once again, year in and year out, we read our people's story. We read of Abraham and Isaac and Jacob, of slavery and freedom, of Exodus and Sinai, of wilderness and Promised Land. And of a good law that makes of us a good people.

Every season and every holiday marking the season teaches us very old lessons that are very new. Celebrating and understanding the great past make us ready to build a good future.

TREASURES OF TRUTH AND WISDOM

Jewish holidays and special seasons show what Jews value: Pesaḥ celebrates freedom; Shavuot the giving of the Law; Sukkot God's care and protection. And Simḥat Torah celebrates the study of God's Law. By celebrating and understanding the past, Jews are helped to build the future.

THE SPECIAL DAYS

As the earth moves about the sun
The seasons change.
Each year, at the same time, the seasons change,
And we mark the holidays of the seasons.

Some important days have nothing to do with the seasons.
They are the days when something happened in history.
A good king died,
A bad king arose.
A nation was built,
A nation was destroyed.
Brave men stood firm for the good and the right.
Sometimes they lost,
We remember and are sad.
Sometimes they won,
We remember and are glad.

Our lives are part of this history,
Part of our people's times,
The good times and the bad,
Times long ago, yesterday, today, tomorrow.
Because the history days were important,
And continue to be important—
They are important to us.
They, too, teach us what we should do with our time.

16

Ḥanukkah

Freedom of worship

Jewish holidays have to do with nature and God, with the growth of crops and the growth of the Jewish people. Only one Jewish holiday—Ḥanukkah—centers about a war. Even that one does not celebrate victory but cleaning the Temple and dedicating it once again.

Jews never take up the sword willingly. No one can take joy in the death of another human being. But sometimes we have no choice. We must stop and fight those who would deny us the freedom to be Jews. If we do not, we are, in effect, agreeing to become slaves.

That's why Mattathias, the priest of Modin, is the real hero of Ḥanukkah. He had the courage to stand up to the Syrians. His son Judah Maccabee was a great general who led the Jews to victory over the Syrians.

Mattathias did not want war. When many people shouted for war, Mattathias ran away from Jerusalem

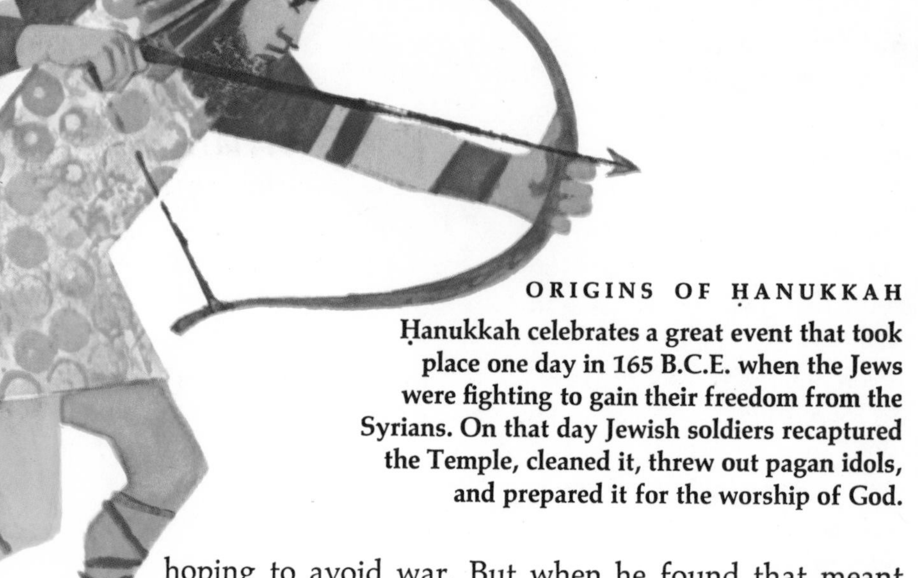

ORIGINS OF ḤANUKKAH

Ḥanukkah celebrates a great event that took place one day in 165 B.C.E. when the Jews were fighting to gain their freedom from the Syrians. On that day Jewish soldiers recaptured the Temple, cleaned it, threw out pagan idols, and prepared it for the worship of God.

hoping to avoid war. But when he found that meant he would have to give up his Judaism he knew what he had to do. If war and death were the price the Jews had to pay for the right to be Jews, then war and death it would be.

Two thousand years before Abraham Lincoln said that a nation cannot endure half slave and half free, Mattathias, the priest of Modin, sent his five sons into war against the Syrians because he knew that the Jews could not exist half slave and half free.

Under foreign rulers

The story of Ḥanukkah really starts about 334 B.C.E. when Alexander the Great conquered all the known world, including the Land of Israel. When Alexander died, his generals split the world into four great empires. One had its capital in Egypt, another in Syria. The Land of Israel lay between them and it was the cause of constant quarrels. The land—and the Jews who lived there—belonged first to Egypt, then to Syria, then to Egypt, and again to Syria.

In 175 B.C.E., Antiochus IV became king of Syria. His father had been the last king to take Judea away from Egypt, and Antiochus was worried that the Egyptians would try to take it back. To strengthen his empire, he tried to unify all the peoples of Syria. But his idea of unity was that everyone follow the same customs. To gain control over the Jews, Antiochus replaced the High Priest with his own man, Joshua, who then took a Greek name, Jason.

Revolt against the Syrians

Even when the young priests and the sons of the rich followed Greek customs and Greek ways of thinking, the Jews remained quiet. But this wasn't enough for Antiochus. In 168 B.C.E. he said everyone under his rule must also worship the Greek god Zeus. He ordered an idol of Zeus be put in the Temple and all Jewish religious rites—circumcision, teaching the Torah, keeping the Shabbat—be punished with death.

When Antiochus' soldiers came to the village of Modin, Mattathias stood firm. The Book of Maccabees (in the Apocrypha) tells what he said:

Even if all the nations within the king's empire listen to him and give up, each its own faith, yet will I and my sons and my brothers follow the Covenant of our fathers. God forbid that we give up the Torah and the Commandments. We will not listen to the king's words, to leave our faith. . . . Let all who will obey the Torah and keep the Commandments follow me.

Mattathias and his sons fought with the Syrian soldiers and drove them from Modin. And the war began.

Mattathias' son Judah gathered together groups of Jews and created an army in the hills of Judea. For three years they fought and beat the Syrians. As winter came in 165 B.C.E., Judah's soldiers entered Jerusalem and then Judah's army came to the Temple. The great stone altar stood there, with a great statue of Zeus—or was it Antiochus?

Cleansing the Temple

The soldiers threw down their arms and began to clean the Temple. The idols were thrown out and everything cleaned. Priests and Levites came forward from among the soldiers, and animals for sacrifices were brought. All was ready for the beginning of services—except for the great menorah. One legend says that then the soldiers found eight iron rods stuck in the walls. They put them together in the shape of a menorah and lit candles in them.

And on the twenty-fifth day of Kislev, exactly three years to the day from the day the Temple was taken over by the Syrians, the Temple services were held. Each soldier waved a palm branch instead of a sword. The Levites sang a psalm: "I praise You, Lord, for You have saved me, and have not let mine enemies rejoice over me." So the Temple was rededicated; it was the first *Ḥanukkah.* (The Hebrew word means "dedicate," or "set aside for a special purpose." Ḥanukkah is the holiday celebrating the dedication or rededication of the Temple.)

It was a miracle that the small nation of Jews could defeat the mighty Syrian Empire, even for a while. Another miracle enabled the Jews to hold on to their victory. Just as Antiochus was about to start an all-out war to retake Jerusalem, he died. His son, who had enough trouble with other people, agreed to peace with the stubborn Jews.

Hasmonean kings

Mattathias' son, Judah, was called ha-Maccabee. We do not know exactly what that means. The name may have come from *makkab,* "the hammer," a common nickname for a great warrior. (One of the great heroes in French history is Charles Martel, Charles the Hammer.) Some think it might have come from the first

REVOLT AND VICTORY

When they lived under Syrian Greek rule, some Jews began to follow Greek ways. But most remained loyal to Jewish laws. When Jewish religious rites were forbidden and a statue of a Greek god was set up in the Temple, the loyal Jews revolted. Mattathias, a priest, defied the Syrians, and his five sons, the Maccabees, led a successful fight against them. With their victory, a new Jewish nation was set up. Its kings were descendants of Mattathias, and were called Hasmoneans from his family name, Hasmon.

letters of the verse from the Book of Exodus: *Mi Chamocha Ba'elim Adonai,* "Who is like You among the gods, O Lord?" But whatever its beginning, may have been, the name Maccabee became a proud title in the story of the Jew.

With the coming of peace, a new independent Jewish nation was set up. Its kings were the descendants of Mattathias, through his sons. They took Mattathias' family name, Hasmon, and so were known as the Hasmonean kings.

Changing times

For many years after the end of that war of independence the Jews celebrated Ḥanukkah. But it was a kind of old soldiers' holiday, when those who fought the war got together and recounted their battles and victories. As these soldiers died, the holiday became less important.

The sons and grandsons of Mattathias died, and new kings ruled the Jews. Like so many kings, they became tyrants. The Jew in the street cursed the Hasmonean tyrants and would not celebrate the holiday of the victory of the Hasmoneans.

The legend of the oil

Then the Hasmonean kings were pushed off the throne by the Romans. Foreigners ruled the Jews and they were cruel. The Jews hated them and wanted to rebel. Now the people began to remember their last fight for freedom, from Antiochus. And they remembered Ḥanukkah. New stories and legends began to grow up around this great victory. That may be when the story about the oil was born. It explained why Ḥanukkah is eight days and not just a week.

A modern explanation has to do with Sukkot. When the soldiers of Judah cleaned out the Temple, they remembered that they had been so busy fighting they had not celebrated Sukkot. They decided to reopen the Temple with a second Sukkot. The second reason is the famous legend given in the Talmud. When the soldiers looked for holy oil to burn in the Temple menorah, they found enough for only one day. They poured it into the menorah and it burned for eight days. As long as it burned they celebrated. And so do we.

Another question about Ḥanukkah was: "Why do we celebrate it by lighting a menorah?" The oil legend of the first Ḥanukkah menorah is one answer; the

LEGENDS OF THE PAST

The holiday of Ḥanukkah became important when the Jews again came under the rule of a cruel master—Rome. They thought back to their last fight for freedom. New legends grew up around the old victory. One was of the oil that burned for eight days. Another told of the soldiers' burning candles on eight iron rods. Both spoke of dedication to God.

spears and torches legend is another. We don't know which one is exactly true. But it doesn't much matter. Sometimes there's more real truth in the legends than in the bare facts of history. Spears into torch-holders, a little holy oil that burns a long time, both these legends tell what Judaism wants: dedication to God.

Ḥanukkah today

No wonder Ḥanukkah has remained an important, though minor, holiday to Jews ever since Roman days. While some special prayers are added to the synagogue service, Ḥanukkah is celebrated mainly in the home, like Pesaḥ, but there is no special feast for it. Even Purim, another minor holiday with few ceremonies, is supposed to end with a special dinner. Why not Ḥanukkah? A Ḥasidic rabbi explained why:

On Purim, he said, we celebrate the ending of a royal command that would have destroyed our bodies. So we celebrate the event with a feast which gives pleasure to our bodies. But on Ḥanukkah we celebrate victory over a royal command that would have destroyed our souls by making us worship an idol. So we celebrate by singing special psalms at services, which gives pleasure to our spirits.

Lighting the menorah

The most important symbol of Ḥanukkah is the menorah. In fact, this holiday was called the Festival of Lights long before it was called the Festival of Dedication.

Lights, candles, rows of lights in menorahs, have always been part of the Jews' religious ritual. When the ancient Hebrews left Egypt and built the Tent of Meeting where the Ark was kept, they also made a grand menorah. The Bible describes it:

. . . a lamp of pure gold; of beaten gold, even its base and its shaft. . . . Let six branches go out of the sides; three branches out of one side; and three branches out of the other side. So (with the middle shaft) it shall have seven lamps. . . .

LIGHT AND JOY

Ḥanukkah is the Festival of Lights. The lights come from the Ḥanukkah menorah which has a candle for each of the eight days, and a shammash candle to light them. Ḥanukkah is a time for playing games and singing, for visiting and giving gifts, especially gifts for the poor.

This was the first *Ner Tamid,* the Eternal Light before the Ark.

Such a seven-branched menorah was for use only in the Temple. It could not be used to mark the Feast of Lights in the home. Instead, a new menorah was fashioned. This one had places for eight lights, one for each night of Ḥanukkah. Then there is another place for the Shammash light. It is called the *Shammash,* the "servant" light, because we use it to light the other lights. We do not want any of the lights celebrating the holiday to be used for anything, not even to light another light. The Ḥanukkah lights are just to make things gay and happy. And we are not supposed to do our regular work while they are burning. Since the rule is that they should last a half hour, that means a half hour of fun and pleasure for the family.

Some people think that just as the three festivals Pesaḥ, Shavuot, and Sukkot celebrate spring, summer, and fall, so Ḥanukkah celebrates the coming of winter. More, it celebrates the days' getting longer. It does so by having lights in the house each night and more and more of them. The disciples of Hillel said it was part of a Jewish idea: with holy things we should always try to do more and more, not less and less.

There are some interesting customs about making a menorah. One says, "All the lights should be on one level because no day is more important than another." Another says, "The Shammash not only must be on another level to show it's not for a night of the holiday, but it should be higher, to show the importance of good work." Today there are many different styles of menorahs. The Israelis call them *Ḥanukkiot* because they use the word *menorah* for "lamp."

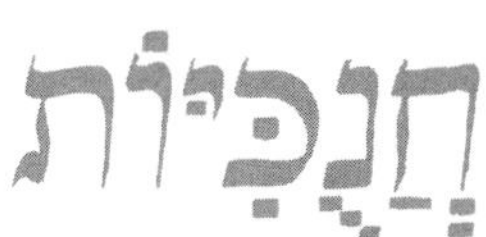

The Ḥanukkah menorah is supposed to be placed so that everyone passing on the street will be reminded of the miracle of Ḥanukkah.

Gifts and giving, songs and games

Ḥanukkah is a festival, a happy holiday. So on that holiday, Jews do those things that give happiness. They give gifts, they sing songs, they play games, they visit.

We do not know how the custom of Ḥanukkah gifts started. Until fairly recently, only money was given on Ḥanukkah—and only on one night. Today, the few coins that were given have grown into elaborate presents, and even to gifts given on every night of the festival. On Ḥanukkah the poor were entitled to special gifts. During that festival they went from house to house and received money for the Feast of Dedication.

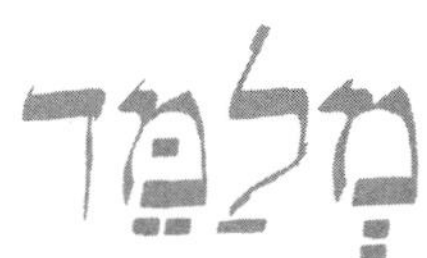

In many Sephardic communities, it was a custom for the *melammed,* the teacher, and his students to go from house to house collecting good things to eat. The melammed collected his pay for the year at the same time. Then the entire class, students and teacher, went back to the schoolroom for a great Ḥanukkah feast.

Spinning the dreidel

Ḥanukkah is a day of joy, the only holiday for which there is a game. It is played with a *dreidel,* a top. This is a four-sided spinner with a Hebrew letter on each side. The letters are *nun, gimel, hey, shin.* They are said to mean *Nes Gadol Hayah Sham,* "A great miracle happened there," referring to the miracle of the oil.

The dreidel is used in a game in which everyone puts some pennies or nuts in the middle of the table. Then each spins the dreidel in turn. If the *nun* turns up, it means *nichts,* or "nothing," and the player gets nothing; if the *gimel* turns up, it means *ganz,* or "all," and the player takes all the money in the pot; if the *hey* turns up, it means *halb,* or "half," and the player takes half; if the *shin* turns up, it means *shtell,* or "put," and he adds to the pot. (The directions are in Yiddish.)

The game is fairly new among Jews. It was probably borrowed from one of the peoples among whom they lived. It was a good way to spend the half hour of joy while the candles burned, and even to continue after.

The right to worship

Today some people try to use Ḥanukkah to show that the Jews were a warrior people. They were not. Most Jews in all ages thought war was stupid. The great men of the Jews were not warriors. They were men of learning, lawgivers, wise men. In a period of about 1,500 years there were only four great generals among the Jews. Two of them are not thought of as generals, Joshua and David. Only Judah Maccabee and Bar Kokhba are remembered as warriors, and they are more important to us today, because our times are so troubled, than they were to the Jewish tradition.

Some people try to change the meaning of Ḥanukkah so that it celebrates a war for independence. It wasn't. The Jews would rather have had their own government and king, but they did not go to war over politics. As a matter of fact, they accepted Antiochus; they accepted his taxes, even when he taxed the Temple. But they would not accept his interference with their worship, their belief, their religion.

MEANING OF ḤANUKKAH

Ḥanukkah is also a Festival of Dedication. It reminds us of the value of freedom of worship. It recalls our dedication to God.

Freedom to serve God

So this war was the first for the right of a people within a country to believe as they wish—so long as they followed the king's law in worldly matters. For thousands of years, Jews have lived under kings, princes, dukes, caliphs, governors, presidents. And they have always been loyal to these rulers—so long as they were permitted to practice their own religion. This idea of religious freedom is followed in all free nations today. It was first given to the world by the Jews.

One thing more: Antiochus offered the Jews complete equality with all the rest of his subjects—so long as they would agree to *be* like all his other subjects. He said: If you Jews become like all my other people, you can enjoy all the rights my other subjects have. So the Jews fought, not for equality, but for the right to be different.

For Jews life is very, very important. But it is not the most important thing. Jews will *not* do *anything* to survive. For some things one must stand up and not give in. The Maccabees risked their lives for freedom to serve God.

That's why the festival of Ḥanukkah does not take place on the day of a great battle. It does not take place on the day the Jews reconquered Jerusalem. It takes place during the week that the Temple was cleansed and a new fire lighted in the menorah. Such a day is so important that it must be celebrated.

17

Tu bi-Shevat

A symbol of life

The Jewish calendar, with all its holidays, is tied to the cycle of growing things. To more than any other green thing, the religion of the Jews is tied to trees, especially to fruit trees. The tree is not just another plant in the Bible; it is the symbol of life, the symbol of man, the symbol of the Jewish people.

עֵץ חַיִּים

According to the Bible, God put two trees in the middle of the Garden of Eden: the tree of knowledge, and the tree of life—*Etz Ḥayyim* (words we use for the Torah rollers).

Although war was a part of everyday life in ancient days, Jews had to follow special rules even in war. The Torah says that Jews cannot make war on trees. When they besieged a city, even if they needed trees to build war machines, they could not cut down fruit trees.

And the prophet Isaiah said, "As the days of a tree, so shall be the days of My people."

The special regard of the Jews for trees may have developed because they lived in a hot climate. There trees are particularly precious. In the wilderness a tree means water, a tree means food, a tree means shade. Any of these may mean life.

Planting trees

And when trees are cut down, the desert creeps in. The Land of Israel was a land of milk and honey in the days of the Bible. It became a land of rocks and sand after the Jews were driven from the land, and the trees were cut down. It is again becoming a land of milk and honey—largely because we have been planting trees there for more than fifty years.

Most plants die in the autumn. They die a natural death or they are cut down for food. New plants appear in the spring to take their place. But trees do not die when the cold rains come. Most lose their leaves and appear to sleep for a few months. But the sturdy trunk stands and the roots, deep underground, hide the life of the tree. In the spring, the tree awakens. This cycle of green and brown, of life and sleep and awakening, goes on year after year. Most trees live much longer than most men. Trees live for fifty, a hundred, even a thousand years. The Jews see in these trees the continuing goodness of God and the continuing duties of man. Man must plant trees and care for them, having faith that God will reawaken the trees each year, long after the men who planted them are dead.

The Talmud tells the story of an old man who was seen planting a carob tree as the king rode by. "Old man," the king called, "how many years will it be before that tree will bear fruit?" "Perhaps seventy years," the old man said. "And how old are you?" the king asked. "Seventy years," the old man replied. "Do you really expect to be alive to eat the fruit of that tree?" the king asked.

THE IMPORTANCE OF TREES
The Jewish calendar is tied to the seasons of growing things. And in the Jewish religion the tree is a symbol of life. Trees are especially important in hot climates like Israel.

"No," the old man said, "but just as I found the world fruitful when I was born, so I plant trees that later generations may eat thereof."

In fact, Jews consider the planting of trees so important that Rabbi Johanan ben Zakkai said: If you should be standing with a young tree in your hand when the Messiah arrives, first finish planting the tree, then go and greet the Messiah.

New Year of the Trees

Shevat, the Hebrew month that comes around February, is the beginning of spring in the Land of Israel. The three months before Shevat—*Ḥeshvan, Kislev, Tevet*—are months when there is much rain. The rains lessen in Shevat; the sun comes out. And the sap begins to rise in the fruit trees. Tiny leaf buds appear on the trees. The dark green of the Israeli winter begins to lighten to the bright greens of spring. Almost overnight, the almond tree, called "the quick one," bursts into white blossoms.

This is a time for rejoicing; a time for celebrating the New Year of the Trees—*Rosh Hashanah Leilanot*. It falls on the fifteenth day of Shevat, it is called *Ḥamishah Asar bi-Shevat*, or *Tu bi-Shevat*. (The Hebrew letters *tet* [9] and *vav* [6], which spell *Tu*, add up to 15.) Six weeks after the winter holiday, Ḥanukkah, it is time to look forward to the coming of spring.

Why does the calendar have a New Year for trees? Because the Torah has a law about them. It says: Do not eat the fruit of a tree during its first three years. The fourth year give its fruit to the priests as a gift to God and thanks for all the tree will bring you. From the fifth year on, you may eat its fruit.

But who can tell on exactly what day a tree is four years old, or five? That's why the 15th day of Shevat is the New Year of trees. On that day, they are all a year older. It's really the birthday we give to the trees.

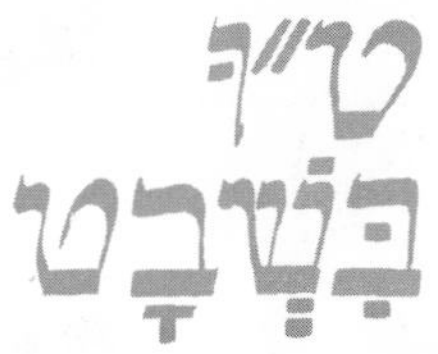

Just as the tree is different from all other growing things, so is its holiday different from all other Jewish holidays. Tu bi-Shevat is not mentioned in the Bible; even the Talmud lists this holiday only as a date in the calendar. There are no special prayers for Tu bi-Shevat in the prayer book. There are no special laws for observing Tu bi-Shevat. It is almost just another day in the calendar. Almost, but not really, for it is the day when we get to show our love not only for the trees but for the Land of Israel. So there are special customs for celebrating this day, some of them quite new.

Old customs

One of the oldest customs is mentioned in the Talmud. It says that on Tu bi-Shevat, a young cedar was planted for every boy born during the year; a young cypress was planted for every girl. And when the young people grew up and came to be married, branches from their cedars and cypresses were cut and woven together to form their *ḥupah.*

We don't know much more about Tu bi-Shevat in olden days. So you might think it would have disappeared from the calendar of Jewish holidays when the Jews were driven from the Land of Israel. In time most Jews found themselves in cold northern climates. There Tu bi-Shevat came in midwinter and there trees were not a matter of life and death. In any case, it was February. Trees were bare on Tu bi-Shevat and the earth was iron-hard.

NEW YEAR, OR BIRTHDAY, OF THE TREES

Since the Bible commands man not to eat the fruit of trees until their fifth year, the Jews had to know the age of the trees. So they gave them all a common "birthday," the 15th of Shevat, when spring is about to begin. Tu bi-Shevat is not mentioned in the Bible. It has no special prayers. But it was an ancient custom to plant a cedar on that day for a new baby boy, a cypress for a girl. And Jews living in other lands remembered Israel by eating the fruits of trees grown there, and giving money to the poor to buy fruit too.

RUTH

JOSHUA

But the Jews did not forget Jerusalem and the Holy Land and the trees. They remembered the Land that had been promised them and from which they were driven; they remembered its trees; they remembered Tu bi-Shevat. The custom grew to celebrate this holiday by eating the fruits that grew in Palestine. They ate figs, dates, raisins, almonds. They ate sweet pods of the carob tree, called *bokser* or "St. John's bread."

They ate the fruit of these and other trees, remembered the Land and recalled its glories.

In some communities, just as the poor were given *maot ḥittim* (money for wheat) on Pesaḥ, so they were given *maot pérot* (money for fruit) on Tu bi-Shevat that they too might have fruit and remember the Holy Land.

Trees for Israel

And that was all Tu bi-Shevat was for centuries: a quiet, pleasant midwinter day when northern Jews remembered. Then the first modern Jewish settlers went to rebuild the Land. They were followed by more waves of Jewish settlers. They wanted to be farmers as well as city people, so some went to till the soil, others to build cities. But the land was dry and rocky. In many places it would not hold water. Its trees had been cut down, so its soil was bad. Again, trees became a symbol of the Jewish people. For trees are as important to the success of Israel as its water, as are factories, as are people. Trees turn the desert into green land, cause water to stay in the earth, feed and shelter people. Trees planted years ago give lumber today.

So Tu bi-Shevat, the New Year of the Trees, became not only the day when trees are again planted in the Holy Land, but the day when their importance to the State of Israel is celebrated.

And the people who are rebuilding the land recognize the importance of trees. The new settlers made Tu bi-Shevat a day to celebrate by planting trees.

Each year now many Israelis, particularly children, plant trees on the sand dunes, in the marshes, or wherever they are needed. They are fulfilling the prophecy of Isaiah:

They shall build up the old ruins.
They shall raise up what was destroyed,
They shall make the destroyed cities new,
And rebuild the ruins of many generations.

All over the world, too, Jews pay for the planting of trees in Israel. The Jewish National Fund makes it possible to give money in our country and know that your tree will be planted where it is needed in Israel.

Trees of remembrance

Because the tree is the symbol of continuing life, it is done in memory of those who died. It's as if their spirits continue in the continuing life of the trees. Often people will get together and plant a whole forest. One of the most famous was begun on Tu bi-Shevat, 1949. A forest was planted in Israel to mark the six million Jews killed by the Nazis. Today there are six million trees planted in this forest along the road to Jerusalem. The trees will be forever green, and our six million brothers will never be forgotten.

REMEMBERING—AND LOOKING AHEAD

The tree, as a symbol of life, is planted in remembrance of those who have died. A special forest of six million trees in Israel recalls the six million Jews killed by the Nazis. A tree also expresses man's faith in the future. Today Tu bi-Shevat not only ties all Jews together—it ties them all to Israel.

That was one forest begun on Tu bi-Shevat. There are many more. And we continue to plant trees—to mark a death and a birth; to celebrate a *simḥah.* But mostly we plant trees on Tu bi-Shevat to show our faith.

We plant trees whose fruit we will not eat. We plant trees in whose shade we will not sit. We plant trees we may never see. We plant them in faith that God will provide the rain and the sun in proper measure for the tree to grow. We plant them in faith that God will see to it that there will be people to eat the fruit and enjoy the shade and welcome the sight of the green trees.

To plant a tree is to say: I believe. I believe that we will overcome our problems. I believe that the world can and will get better. I believe that the day will come when, as the Bible says, everyone will be able to sit under his own fig tree and be unafraid. The man who fears that the world will end tomorrow, or next year, does not plant trees.

On Tu bi-Shevat we celebrate the New Year of the Trees and our own belief in the future of the world. On Tu bi-Shevat, tied so closely to Israel and its feasts, we celebrate the unbreakable bonds between Jews everywhere and the Land of Israel. On Tu bi-Shevat we mark the oneness of the Jewish people.

18
Purim

Being loyal to others

Most of us want to be famous or important even though we haven't yet earned the right. Wanting these things is all right. The wanting makes us work hard to get them. The problem is: What would we do, what would we give up to get what we want?

Would we cheat to get to the head of the class?

Would we turn away from our friends to get in with more popular people?

Would we break the rules set by our parents to show we're not afraid?

Would we turn away from the Jewish people to try to be more successful?

For twenty centuries, most Jews lived among people who hated them. Only a very few ever achieved success and positions of power. Often these successful ones forgot their fellow Jews. Or tried to. But some who reached positions of power never forgot their peo-

THE BOOK OF ESTHER

Probably the events as told in the Book of Esther did not take place. But even if the story is not fact it contains great truth. Throughout the centuries, in keeping with that truth, loyal Jews, fortunate themselves, have reached out to protect and befriend Jews who were poor, persecuted, and in danger.

ple. They were willing to help, even if it meant risking their power and riches.

That, as much as anything, is what Purim is about.

Esther did not think about her people when she became a queen—but she could not forget them. Mordecai would not let Esther forget.

The holiday of Purim celebrates the Jews who always remember the people from whom they came. It celebrates those who, having forgotten for a while, remember and help.

פּוּרִים

Our people might not have been able to live through the many dark centuries, if not for such people and the God who has given us a few brave Jews in every generation. It is in their stories, in each "miracle" of Jews escaping death, that the Jews see proof that God still wants them to continue working along His way.

The story of Esther

Purim is a very odd holiday. Things seem to be turned upside down. The synagogue, in which we are quiet on every other day of the year, becomes a place for noise. The book of the Bible that tells the story of Purim, the Book of Esther, is different from all the other books. It never mentions God.

Its story has four main characters: King Ahasuerus, Queen Esther, Haman, and Mordecai. Ahasuerus, king of Persia, was displeased with his queen, Vashti, had her removed and married Esther, a Jewish girl.

The king's chief minister was Haman, who hated Jews. Haman got the king to let him have all the Jews killed. Haman had his magicians choose a lucky day for this evil act. The magicians chose the day by casting lots—*pur* in Persian, from which we get the word *Purim*. They probably used colored sticks or stones to find just the right day.

Mordecai, Queen Esther's cousin, asked her to plead with the king to save her people. But the rule of the Persian court was that no one could come before the king unless asked to do so. The punishment for breaking the rule was death. So Esther was afraid to approach Ahasuerus, but she went. The king loved her, so he listened to her and hanged Haman and all his friends.

On the day the Jews were supposed to have been wiped out, the 14th day of Adar, we celebrate the saving of the Jews of Persia as the Feast of Purim. It comes a month after Tu bi-Shevat (unless there is a Jewish leap year) and a month before Pesaḥ

LOYALTY TO OUR OWN

Jews value loyalty. Purim celebrates the saving of the Persian Jews from certain death through the loyalty and high courage of a Jewish girl, the queen of King Ahasuerus. And Jews see in this story something of God's way of working things out.

Stories with meaning

Most of the books of the Bible are based on actual events. The Hebrews did conquer the Land of Israel. There was a King David and a King Solomon, an Isaiah and an Ezekiel. However, some scholars feel that the story of Esther never took place. But those events are still true. They happened in real life in many times, in many places. Jews were often in danger because of a king or prince or lord. At the last moment some miracle occurred and the Jews were saved. So though the story of Esther may not have happened in that time at that place to those people, it is real, nevertheless. Only the names and places have been changed.

The power of God

The Book of Esther is unusual because the story is told in much the same way as modern detective stories, with good guys and bad guys. The powerful people are about to wipe out the weak people. A leader of the powerful group, or his son, falls in love with a beautiful woman of the weak people. She gets her lover to save her people.

But the Jews added something to this well-known plot. It did not need to be mentioned. Everybody understood. The Jews saw in this story not the accident of two people falling in love, but God's way of working things out in history. He keeps His promise not to let the Jewish people die.

Because it celebrates the saving of the Jews, Purim has become a favorite holiday even if it is a minor one.

Loyalty among the Jews

If the Jews had been able to live peacefully in their own land, Purim might have disappeared. But the Jews were spread throughout the world. They lived in lands where new Hamans kept arising. The Purim story gave the Jews courage and hope. It taught them that God would not permit the Jews to be destroyed; some miracle would save a portion of the people, if not every single Jew. And it taught them that in a crisis all Jews were one people. When the people were threatened, even the rich and powerful, even the advisers to kings, joined the poor and humble Jews to fight for the existence of the Jewish people.

New Purims

Since the events told in the Purim story kept repeating, Jews marked similar escapes by new Purims. Many towns and provinces have their own little Purims to celebrate their deliverances.

In Spain, in the fourteenth century, a knight named Gonzalo became adviser to the king of Castile. He hated the Jews and plotted against them. Castile was at war with Portugal, and as in all wars, much money was needed. Gonzalo suggested to the king of Castile that if the Jews were driven from Castile, the king could take away all their land and riches. The king

NEW PURIMS

There have been many real-life variations on the story we read in Esther. Some of these occasions when Jews were saved are celebrated in "little Purims." Moroccan Jews in some towns even celebrate the saving of Portuguese Christian enemies. To Jews every human life is unique and to be valued.

agreed, and the Jews of Castile were marked for expulsion.

Another of the king's advisers was Moses Abudiel, a Jew. He tried to get the king to revoke the order for expulsion but was not successful—until he got the help of the king's beloved, Leonora de Guzman. Together, Moses and Leonora worked to save the Jews.

This story, so like that of Esther, was celebrated in a holiday called the Purim of Castile.

The Jews were not welcome in the Land of Israel during the centuries that Palestine was a Turkish province. But early in the 1700's the sheik who governed the city of Tiberias invited a community of Jews to live there. No sooner had the Jews settled down when Suleiman Pasha, governor of Damascus, decided the sheik had gone too far. When the sheik refused to drive out the Jews, Suleiman Pasha besieged Tiberias.

For 83 days the city was cut off. There was no food and no weapons to continue the fight. Suddenly, the pasha withdrew his armies. But the withdrawal was only a trick to rouse the hopes of the Tiberians. Suleiman Pasha's armies surrounded the city again. This time there seemed to be no hope. But just as the sheik was about to give in, Suleiman Pasha dropped dead. Tiberias—and its Jews—were saved.

To this day the Jews of Tiberias celebrate their own, extra Purim.

Fasts, feasts, and gladness

The Purim holiday begins, in a way, on the day before. Remember, Esther could not appear before the king unless he had sent for her, or she might be killed. To ask God's help in her brave act, Esther and all the Jews of Shushan fasted for three days. In memory of Esther's courage, the day before Purim is officially a fast day, the Fast of Esther. Some Jews still observe this in modern times.

PURIM IN THE SYNAGOGUE

The Book of Esther is read at the evening and morning services in the synagogue service on Purim. When the reader comes to the name of the wicked Haman we drown out his name with the sound of our noisemakers.

The Book of Esther commands us to celebrate Purim as "days of feasting and gladness, and of sending gifts to one another, and gifts to the poor." There is no mention of resting or services. So Purim is a holiday on which work can be done. And of course we celebrate the victory of good over evil in the synagogue.

The service on the eve of Purim is the regular daily evening service, with the addition of some special prayers and blessings. But at both the evening service and the morning service the Megillah is read. *Megillah* means "scroll." There are five books of the Bible that were often written as separate scrolls. These are the five Megillot, each one read at different times: Esther, read on Purim; Song of Songs, read on Pesaḥ; Ruth, read on Shavuot; Lamentations, read on Tisha be-Av; and Ecclesiastes, read on Sukkot. All of these books are called Megillot, but when someone says, "the Megillah," he means the Megillah of Esther, which is read on Purim. No reading in the synagogue is like that one!

During the reading of the Megillah, the rules that govern synagogue behavior all the rest of the year are forgotten.

When the name of Haman is read in the Megillah it is the custom to drown it out with noise. Everyone turns a *grager* (noisemaker) or scrapes his feet, to keep the name of this hater of the Jews from being heard again among men. It seems a strange custom. But it teaches an important lesson. Haman was our enemy. How do we Jews get even with him? We do not call him names. We do not attack people who look like him or remind us of him. We simply take away his place in history. We destroy his memory. We make him a nothing—by refusing to hear his name. And by standing up for truth and right for all men.

Gifts of food

The second part of the rule about celebrating Purim says we must send gifts one to another, *shalaḥ-manot*, and that came to mean gifts of food. This is a very old custom; it began even before Purim became a holiday. For example, the Bible says that when Ezra read the Torah to the Jews of Jerusalem there was great joy. And the occasion was marked by sending shalaḥ-manot. The idea is a nice one, and today we still give gifts of food on many holidays and celebrations.

Gifts to the poor

The third part of the Purim rule says that we must "give gifts to the poor." Since it says "gifts" and not "gift," the Rabbis said we must give to at least two

FUN AND GAMES—AND LOVINGKINDNESS

Purim is a regular working day. But we celebrate at home with games and singing and gift-giving. And we give to the poor. Purim balls and masquerades raise money for charity.

poor persons. And even the poor person who receives gifts on Purim is supposed to give gifts, in turn, to others of the poor. Sharing is so important that everyone ought to do it.

The Ḥasidic rabbi of the town of Paris used to call all the poor of the town to his door on the day after Purim and give them food and money. He explained that everyone was so busy giving charity on Purim that they never thought of giving to the poor the next day. But the poor need help every day. So he saved part of his charity for the day after Purim.

This tradition of personal giving is very hard to follow in large cities. So we have developed other ways of following the law of charity—not only on Purim but throughout the year.

Plays, balls, and carnivals

The custom of masquerading and putting on plays on Purim is fairly new—for Jews. It is only about four hundred years old. It was probably taken over from the Christian custom of masquerading during the week before Lent, and particularly on the day before Lent begins—Mardi Gras. This day comes about the same time as Purim.

This carefree playing was often given a special meaning by the Jews when the Purim *shpiel* (play) raised money for charity. More than a hundred years ago, the Jews of New York organized the Purim Association. The Association ran a great Purim ball every year. That gave everyone an opportunity to celebrate with feasting and gladness—and raised large amounts of money for Jewish institutions and charities. Out of this Purim Association grew today's New York Federation of Jewish Philanthropies, the largest one-city charity organization in the world.

Even today, in many communities, Purim plays and carnivals are used to raise money for Jewish causes.

The Purim-rabbi Long before there were Purim plays there were other ways of having fun in honor of Purim. One was the custom of naming a Purim-rabbi of the town. He was chosen from among the brightest of the students in the school. He served for one day, on Purim. But that day the Purim-rabbi had the right to make jokes about anyone and anything. And he did. Through the Purim-rabbi, the Jews made fun of their troubles, made fun of the powerful, made fun of the most solemn parts of their lives.

Jewish literature of the last three hundred years has a special Jewish humor. It is bitter-funny, tearful-funny. But it is funny. Most of this humor is not against other peoples. We make fun mostly of ourselves.

This looking at ourselves and our troubles with laughter as well as with tears may have begun in the Purim celebrations.

Survival of the people On this holiday we say: If things are good, be joyful. If things are bad, they'll get better; so be joyful. And if things are very bad, perhaps a miracle may save us. This doesn't mean that the Jews were always saved. They weren't. There was no Purim for the Jews of Europe during the Nazi period. But even though millions of Jews died, the Jewish people survived. We are still sad over the frightful suffering of our people then. We are still not sure how men could be so evil. But we also know that just being sad is not enough. We must not let Hitler and people like him keep us from living life, from working to bring the Days of the Messiah. So each year when we go to the synagogue on Purim we are a little sad—but when we see all the Jews still there, not defeated, serving God, wanting to build a good world, we are happy. Happy for all the Mordecais and Esthers that were and will yet be.

19

Tisha be-Av

Remembering bad times

Life is not all parties and feasts. Nor would we want it to be. And the year of the Jew is not only one happy day after another. There are days of sorrow, too.

There are days when we remember the tragedies, the sad things that happened to us. As we remember and celebrate the Exodus, the gift of the Torah, the saving of the Jews of Persia, so we remember and mark the deaths of great leaders, the destruction of our Temples.

There are times in our personal lives when everything seems to go badly, times when it seems that nothing will ever go right again. But these times pass. And when they do, we try to forget the pain we felt during that period. It is the same with nations as with individuals. Nations, too, try to forget the painful past.

But the remembrance of bad times may be as important as the memory of good times. When we look at the sad past, the present may not be as bad as we thought.

In our long history, there were times when the Jews wanted to give up. They despaired of everything they hoped for—for themselves and for all mankind. There were times when it appeared the long line of the generations of Jews was ended; that there would be no Jews left in all the world in the next generation. But there were always some Jews who did not despair. They remembered the covenant with God and did not give up hoping. Then they knew that God would keep His message alive in them and through them.

So when the bad times passed, Jews reminded each other of what they had lived through and overcome. These memories taught them not to be too proud. It also taught them they could not ignore God for long.

If you remember that we were all once slaves, you cannot be too proud that some of us now govern nations and lead armies and hold great fortunes.

Lessons from the past

If you remember that Jerusalem and the Temple were destroyed, the Jewish nation wiped out, and the Jewish kings and princes taken in chains to Babylon, you cannot say, "I'll do whatever I want, worship anything I want, and nothing will happen to me."

In remembering the whole past—the good and the bad—Jews learned to appreciate what they had. Knowing that their people had almost been wiped out of history, again and again, they were happy to be alive, happy to be here now. So by keeping them alive, God gave to the Jews the gift of the present time. And that also meant the future, for to be a Jew is to care about building God's Kingdom on earth.

Why we fast

Remembering the good past is easy—you feast and have a joyous celebration. Remembering the sad past is harder. Jews, like people everywhere, mark their days of sorrowful remembrance by fasting.

THE FAST DAYS

We remember days of sorrow and defeat as well as days of gladness. Fast days help us recall and understand the hardships of Jews in the past. And fasting helps us feel for those who are in need today.

Two things are absolutely essential to life: air to breathe and food to eat. We cannot give up breathing because death would follow immediately. But we can give up the other essential to life—food—for a time. By so doing, we are, in a small way, putting our lives directly in the hands of God.

We do not fast for God; He gets nothing out of our giving up the pleasure of eating. We fast for ourselves. When we fast, we feel the pain of hunger. When we fast we live through the fear that is caused by hunger, even though we are sure that it will pass. In so doing, we force our bodies to feel, and our minds to remember, a little of what our ancestors underwent in much greater measure long ago.

But it isn't only to remember the past that we fast. Fasting also makes us feel a little of the pain and hunger of those who live in darkness and pain today—on the other side of the world, on the other side of the continent, on the other side of town.

It has been said that "After a man eats and drinks, he has but one heart—for himself alone. Before a man eats and drinks [when he is fasting] he has two hearts—one for himself and one for all the hungry."

When you are full, you cannot really feel the hardship of your poor neighbor. But the person who has not eaten or drunk, who is fasting, feels not only the faintness of his own heart, but also that of others.

So the result of fasting is *tzedakah*, righteousness. We do not fast to punish ourselves. We fast to be able to understand fully the commandment to give bread to the hungry and give shelter to the homeless.

Fast days

The Jewish calendar has four fast days—in addition to Yom Kippur and the Fast of Esther. The four mark sad events in Jewish history. They are the 10th of Tevet, the 17th of Tammuz, the 9th of Av, and the 3rd of Tishri. Each of these is connected in some way with the destruction of the Temple in Jerusalem.

On the Tenth of Tevet, 586 B.C.E., the Babylonian emperor Nebuchadnezzar laid siege to the city of Jerusalem.

On the Seventeenth of Tammuz, the Babylonians made the first break in the walls of besieged Jerusalem.

On the Ninth of Av the destruction of the First Temple, which Solomon had built 400 years before to the glory of God, is commemorated; also the Second Temple was overrun and destroyed by the Romans on that same day in 70 C.E.

On the Third of Tishri, Gedaliah, Jewish governor of Judah, was assassinated.

History of Tisha be-Av

Of these four fasts, Tisha be-Av, the ninth day of Av, is the one most remembered, the most important—even though the Temple was not actually destroyed on that date. The Bible gives two dates for the destruction, the seventh and the tenth of Av. However, we remember that event on a day between the seventh and tenth because on the ninth of Av, Tisha be-Av, bad things have happened to the Jews for thousands of years:

The Second Temple was overrun and destroyed by the Romans on Tisha be-Av in 70 C.E.

Bar Kokhba's fortress of Bettar fell to the Romans on Tisha be-Av in 135 C.E., ending the last revolt of the Jews.

On Tisha be-Av one year later, the Romans plowed under the stones of Jerusalem and began building a Roman city on that holy spot.

In 1492, the Jews were ordered expelled from Spain; on Tisha be-Av more than one hundred thousand Spanish Jews were herded aboard ships to be taken to Africa and the East.

And on Tisha be-Av, 1929, the first serious Arab riot broke out in Jerusalem, beginning the bitter, continuing Arab-Jewish quarrel over the land that was to become Israel.

With that history, it is not surprising that the ninth of Av symbolizes to the Jews every misfortune that befell the people for 2,500 years.

People generally do not have to be reminded of joyous holidays. While happy holidays may change, they seldom die out. Days of mourning are harder to

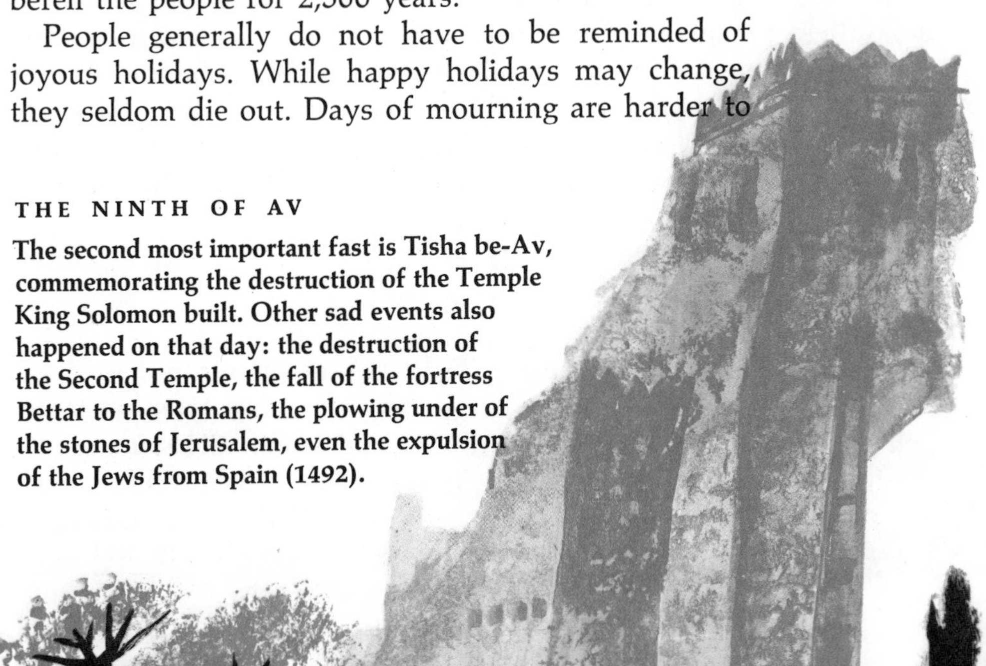

THE NINTH OF AV

The second most important fast is Tisha be-Av, commemorating the destruction of the Temple King Solomon built. Other sad events also happened on that day: the destruction of the Second Temple, the fall of the fortress Bettar to the Romans, the plowing under of the stones of Jerusalem, even the expulsion of the Jews from Spain (1492).

remember year in and year out. Still, the Jews have held tightly to Tisha be-Av. About the year 200, Rabbi Judah Ha-Nasi, the man who collected the Mishnah, tried to end the celebration of Tisha be-Av as a day of mourning. But the people would not follow even that great religious leader; they insisted on observing the fast day. In the years that followed, Tisha be-Av was very strictly observed in some centuries and places, and less strictly observed in others. It was never forgotten. In recent years with the State of Israel alive and growing, with all of Jerusalem under Jewish control for the first time in two thousand years, many people have said Tisha be-Av as a sad day makes no sense. Yet it is still an important day of sadness to anyone who follows traditional Jewish Law. Even in the State of Israel and in front of the great Western Wall in Jerusalem, many Jews will observe the day with great sorrow.

A time of mourning and sorrow

In our grandfathers' time and before, the period of mourning for the lost Temples and the lost homeland began on the fast of the Seventeenth of Tammuz, three weeks before Tisha be-Av, about the middle of the summer. From that day until after Tisha be-Av, the entire Jewish community went about as if there had been a

HOPE OF THE MESSIAH

For Jews there is no sorrow without hope. Legend says that the Messiah will be born on Tisha be-Av. And that lends hope to the day.

death in the family. There were no celebrations, no marriages, no cutting of the hair, no wearing of new clothing. And beginning with the first day of Av, the mourning became deeper. Regular lessons in the schools were put aside. (The rest of the summer, students studied. There were no summer vacations.) The children spent all their time studying the Book of Lamentations. A tradition says that Jeremiah wrote these poems about the destruction of the First Temple.

On the Shabbat before Tisha be-Av, the reading from the Prophets is Isaiah, Chapter 1. There Isaiah tells of the dreadful things that will happen to the Jews for not being good to the poor and needy. That Haftarah reading begins, "The vision of Isaiah . . ." And so that Shabbat is called Shabbat Ḥazon (vision).

הַפְטָרָה

On the eve of Tisha be-Av, the synagogue was like the house of death. The richly decorated curtains of the Ark and the mantles of the Torah were covered with black cloth. The lights were dimmed or put out entirely, except for the light in front of the Ark. The people wore no shoes and sat on boxes or on the floor as in a house of mourning. And the Book of Lamentations was chanted to an especially sad melody.

Services on the day of Tisha be-Av began very early and ended late. At the morning service the men did not wear their prayer shawls nor did they put on Tefillin; they waited until the afternoon service to put these on.

The light of hope

But for Jews even the most terrible grief must end on a happy note. With the end of Tisha be-Av, the Jews are reminded of another ancient legend—the Messiah will be born on Tisha be-Av. So too the Haftarah readings for the weeks following Tisha be-Av are all messages of God's love and care for the Jews. The one on the first Shabbat after Tisha be-Av begins "Bring comfort, bring comfort to My people . . ." So it is called *Shabbat Naḥamu*, the Shabbat of comforting.

This cycle of sorrow and comfort, of pain and joy, reminds us once again that life is precious and must go on. In times of sorrow and mourning, life somewhat slows up. So these times must be limited; we cannot sorrow and mourn too long. And after the mourning we begin to live fully once again.

Although the two great fast days—Yom Kippur and Tisha be-Av—have always had a very strong hold on the imagination of the Jews, there has also been a healthy limit to fasting and other such practices. (Some religions encourage people to punish their body for the good of their soul. That is not the Jewish attitude.)

Duties to our fellow man

One of the Ḥasidic rabbis, the Sassover Rebbe, said: "If your neighbor offends you, and you hold back your anger, it is more pleasing to God than a thousand fasts."

The Rabbis of the Talmud also said there was a strong connection between Tisha be-Av and man's duty to his fellow man. They asked why the First Temple was destroyed. The answer was that it was punishment. The Jews were guilty of worshiping idols, of murder, and other crimes. Then why, they asked, was the Second Temple destroyed? And the answer was that in those days the people hated each other without reason. This teaches us, the Rabbis said, that hatred of your fellow man is as bad as murder and idolatry.

A Ḥasidic Rebbe once came to a town on the eve of Tisha be-Av. A bitter quarrel had split the Jews of this town, and the town's rabbi asked the visiting Bershider Rebbe to act as peacemaker. "But," said the town rabbi, "you will of course want to wait until after Tisha be-Av before beginning your efforts." "No," said the Bershider Rebbe, "the Second Temple was destroyed because men hated each other without cause. What better way to mark Tisha be-Av than to try to end hatred in this town?"

LESSONS AND DUTIES

Tisha be-Av reminds us that the First Temple is said to have been destroyed because of idol-worshiping and crimes of the Jews; the Second because the people hated each other without cause. The Rabbis teach us to lay aside anger and hatred. We find lessons in sad events even when we cannot understand them.

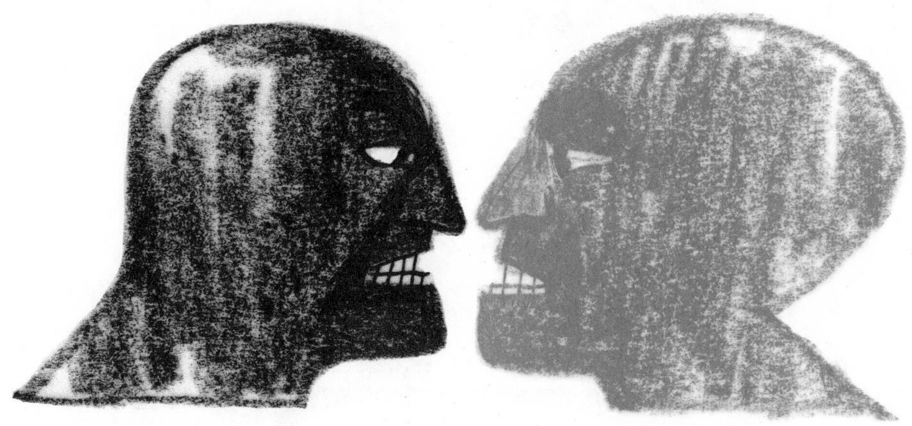

We do not understand why the terrible things we mourn on Tisha be-Av happened to the Jews. We do not understand why God allowed them to happen. In the same way we do not understand why sad things happen to us or to our families. But as we look back, particularly when we get older, over the history of our people, something often becomes clear: In suffering, and through the memory of suffering on days like Tisha be-Av, we find out many things it is impossible to learn in joy. And we are better for it.

We may not be able to find a reason for everything that happens. But Jews have been able to find a lesson in almost everything that happens, and that has helped them become good people. The whole Jewish calendar, the whole Jewish sense of time, is a series of lessons about life.

THE YEARS

Seven days go by—and it is a week.
Four weeks pass—and it is a month.
Three months come and go—and it is a season.
The four seasons pass—it is a year.

Once we were babies, carried and fed.
A few years passed and we were small children,
Playing all day long.
More years and we were old enough for school;
We learned to read and write and think.
In the years ahead
We will become men and women,
Take our place in the world,
Marry and have children,
And teach them of the world and time.

What have we done with our years—and what
will we do?
What has made our years good?
And what shall we do to make the future bright?

20

The Days of Awe

Thinking things over

Most holidays are either joyous or sad. They celebrate a victory or a good harvest; they recall the destruction of the Temple. But there are other holidays that are neither full of joy nor of sadness. Their mood is serious, thoughtful. These are the holidays when we look inside ourselves rather than outside at the world. These are the times when we think about what we have been doing with our lives.

The most important of these holidays is not a holiday at all. It is a period of time; it is ten days and the days of preparation for those ten days. We call these ten days—which include two holidays and a fast day and a special Shabbat, the Days of Awe—*Yamim Noraim*.

All of us need times to be serious about ourselves. We need time out from doing things, from being busy, to see where we've been going and where we ought to go. Once each year, a Jew stands back from the round of ordinary days and Sabbaths and asks: What use have I made of my time? Have I used it well or badly?

Such times of being away from things and people are important, particularly when we are growing up. Some years we need to be by ourselves more than with other people. Some years we feel lost if we're not doing things with friends. The quiet, thoughtful times are as important to growing up as the noisy, busy years.

The Days of Awe begin with Rosh Hashanah and end with Yom Kippur. They begin with the celebration of the New Year and end with a day of promise. It is not a time to be afraid or very joyous. It is a time of remembering and thinking, a time of measuring what we did last year so we can do better next year.

Deciding to do better

It's true that many people no longer pay much attention to this period of remembering and thinking. They attend services on Rosh Hashanah and Yom Kippur but they do not bother with the days before and the days between. They are too busy. But the busier people are, the more they need to know where the years are

Yom Kippur thoughts:

1

A CHANCE TO CHANGE

Man is responsible for what he does and how he spends his time. At the New Year he can look back, see what he has been doing, and decide how to do better.

2

3

4

going. If we forget the years that have gone by, we cannot understand ourselves. At the beginning of each year we need to spend some time close to God, to measure the past according to His rules, to plan the future according to what He wants of us.

The Jewish attitude to life and time is given in the other name for this period. The first ten days of the New Year are also called *Aseret Yemé Teshuvah*, the Ten Days of Repentance. A legend explains it: On Rosh Hashanah, each person's acts during the past year are judged. His future is then decided according to the worth of that past and it is written down in the great Book of Life. But the Book of Life for the new year is not closed on Rosh Hashanah. It is left open for ten days, through Yom Kippur. In the days between, every one has the opportunity to change the judgment written in the Book. Each person, our religion teaches, has it within his own power to decide his own future. He doesn't need a saint or a priest or a rabbi to do it for him. It is between him and God. No one, Judaism teaches, is so bad that he cannot change for the better, or so good that he cannot become better.

The judgments of God

Our Rabbis taught that on Rosh Hashanah each man is judged by God. His good deeds are measured against his bad deeds—sins—and he is found guilty or not guilty. So all year long a man should think of himself as being exactly half guilty and half innocent. If he does only one more bad deed, he will be more guilty than innocent. But if he does one more good deed, he will be more innocent than guilty.

Most people today don't like to talk about sin. Even parents and rabbis seldom use this word. But it is a good and important word. It means doing an evil, a bad deed. It means not doing the right thing when you have the opportunity to do so. Some sins are very

obvious—murder, for example. Some are not so obvious —a person is hurt or cries for help; you go by, making believe you do not see him. This—doing nothing—is sometimes a worse sin than doing something a little wrong.

What makes *sin* a word we still need is that it has to do with God. Sin is not doing what God wants you to do. This makes sin more than a mistake; it is an insult to Him. In a way, it's like deliberately doing the opposite of what your parents want you to do. That's why sin makes you feel bad and guilty. If you care about God you will want to do what He expects you to do. When you don't do it you will be ashamed to talk to Him. That is where repentance starts.

Sins to avoid Maimonides, the wisest scholar of his time, liked to have everything in order. He made a list of the 13 things he thought a Jew must believe; he made a list of 8 types of charity; he explained all the Jewish laws in 14 books; he made a list of the 613 commandments.

A TIME TO BE SERIOUS

The Ten Days of Repentance, or Days of Awe, come at the start of the New Year. They begin with Rosh Hashanah and end with Yom Kippur.

And he made a list of 24 acts that keep a person from turning wholeheartedly to God. Studying Maimonides' list gives a good idea of what Jews think about error.

The four worst acts, according to Maimonides, are these: leading a community to do evil; turning another person from good to evil; not correcting a child who is doing wrong; saying to yourself: sure I'll do this, but it won't count because I'll atone for it on Yom Kippur.

These are the worst acts, says Maimonides, because the first three lead to the spoiling, not of your life, but of the lives of others. The last one plays games, not only with good and evil, but with God Himself.

The next worst, says Maimonides, are leaving the community of Jews; opposing the teachings of our Rabbis and Prophets; mocking the commandments; despising teachers; and fighting against correction.

These all have to do with the first step in avoiding error—knowing what it is. To avoid it, you must know the difference between right and wrong. Not any right and wrong, but the Jewish idea of right and wrong. To some people it is very important that you know which fork to use for fish and which for meat, but not whether you have helped the sick or the old or the needy. Jews care more about people than that. In some societies it is all right to pay a priest to do your praying for you, to observe the commandments for you; among Jews each man talks to God for himself.

So to avoid error, you must know what it is. This requires being part of the Jewish community, understanding the laws and teachings of the Jews, giving the teachers their proper place and authority.

The third group of acts in Maimonides' list includes accepting something you know has been stolen; finding something and not really trying to return it; stealing from the poor and the orphaned; taking a bribe to corrupt justice.

These acts are especially evil because the person sinned against cannot be found and so the evil cannot be corrected. For example, if you accept something that has been stolen, you will probably not know from whom it was stolen and so cannot return it. If you find something and do not really try to take it back, you will never know to whom it belonged. And to give a policeman or a judge a bribe is to corrupt him so that justice will be denied another person in the future. You will never know about that injustice or to whom it was done.

The fourth group of acts is being a guest for a meal in a house in which there isn't enough food for the family; using the goods or tools of a poor man; trying to get ahead by pushing someone else back; and being suspicious of innocent people.

These are bad because they seem so unimportant at the moment and the person imagines he hasn't done anything wrong. He doesn't really notice that his food is taken from the plates of the others. He doesn't notice the danger of breaking the poor man's only tool by which he makes a living.

The last group of acts is important because they're the easiest to fall into: gossiping, bad temper, evil thoughts, and bad company.

The fact that a person commits one of these acts does not mean that he is bad or evil. Everyone errs—in small ways or in large. We do this by not thinking or because we are afraid, or because we want things badly. Some people do it out of a sickness of the mind, or because they have been so deeply hurt that they can no longer see right from wrong. We are not perfect, though no one should use that as an excuse to do wrong. Nor should that keep us from trying to become perfect. We cannot succeed in that, but we should try. It's a good way to try to keep getting better.

Nor does God expect us to be perfect, never to do wrong. A Midrash tells of the king's son who was far from his father's palace and had stayed away a long time. One day the son received a message saying that his father wanted to see him. He said: "There's no sense even starting out. It's too far to go and I've been away too long." But his father said: "Go as far as you can son; I shall come the rest of the way to meet you." So it is with God. He says, "Return to Me, My children, and I shall come to meet you."

Seeking God's mercy

Jews begin to prepare themselves for the Days of Awe several weeks before Rosh Hashanah. It is usual for people to want to clean up for a new day, for a new school term, for a new job—and for a new year.

Making a new start

For Jews, the time before and during the Days of Awe are a kind of cleaning up for the new year—a sort of person-cleaning-up time. We translate the Hebrew words *Aseret Yemé Teshuvah* as "the Ten Days of Repentance." They could also be translated as "the Ten Days of Return." This is the time for man to return to God and His way. He may have strayed from that path during the year; now he has an opportunity to return to the right road.

The Bible doesn't say anything about this period, but man's normal wish to clean up before the new year, to rethink his life and his way, makes this preparation for the new year natural.

THE BOOK OF LIFE

The Rabbis taught that by repentance during the Ten Days of Repentance man could even change the judgment of God, written in the Book of Life on Rosh Hashanah. God is merciful and if we draw near to Him, He draws near to us.

In the old days, Jewish courts did not take cases during the month of Tishri so that no man could sue his neighbor and so start a new quarrel in this season. And many people go to the cemetery to visit the graves of their dead during the month of Elul, right before the New Year. They expected so much of us and we still want to be true to them. So we remember, and promise ourselves we will try to be better.

Asking forgiveness

Beginning on the Sunday before Rosh Hashanah, and continuing through the Days of Awe to Yom Kippur, special prayers are said in the synagogue. These are called *Seliḥot*, prayers of forgiveness. These sad and solemn prayers are very old; some go back 1,400 or 1,500 years. Many were written during periods of great persecution. For instance, some of the most moving were written during the time of the Crusades, when the Crusaders killed far more Jews than Moslems, whom they were supposed to be fighting.

The seven days that actually divide the two days of Rosh Hashanah from Yom Kippur begin with a fast—the Fast of Gedaliah. This day marks the death of Gedaliah, a governor who tried to rebuild the nation of Judah after the destruction of the First Temple.

The Shabbat between Rosh Hashanah and Yom Kippur is naturally very special. The whole Shabbat can be made a time to think about one's life; the day is called *Shabbat Shuvah*—the Sabbath of Return. The name comes from the Haftarah read on that Shabbat. The Haftarah is from Hosea and begins, "Return, O Israel, unto the Lord thy God." (Notice that *teshuvah*, repentance, comes from *shuvah*, return.)

One of the old customs of the Days of Awe has, unfortunately, become almost impossible for us. This was the custom of going to all your friends and neighbors and asking forgiveness of those you have wronged.

PREPARING FOR THE NEW YEAR

Traditionally Jews prepare for the New Year even before the Days of Awe. From the Sabbath before Rosh Hashanah on through Yom Kippur special prayers for forgiveness are said in the synagogue. The Sabbath between Rosh Hashanah and Yom Kippur is called the Sabbath of Return—to God. In earlier times, in some European towns, Jews went to each other to ask forgiveness and set things right if need be. They forgave others too. To forgive and be forgiven is to start the New Year fresh.

In the little towns in which most of our grandparents or great-grandparents lived in Europe, people would take time during the Days of Awe to go ask everyone to forgive them if they had wronged them.

All the little, and sometimes the big, wrongs that had been done in the community were brought out into the open, confessed, made good if possible, and forgiven. The entire community felt clean, pure.

Perhaps not everyone was that honest. Not all Jews had the courage to beg someone's pardon or, when they themselves were asked, to give pardon with full hearts. But they found it a lot easier to do than we would. We know a lot more today than they did but we don't know as well as they did how to say to someone, "I'm sorry I was unkind to you." We do many things they never could have dreamed of doing. But they went to friends and almost strangers to admit they had been foolish.

Maybe our biggest sin is that we don't want to admit we sin. Or is it that we can't talk to each other about the wrong we do, each man to his neighbor?

21

Rosh Hashanah

In the Rosh Hashanah prayers we say, as we do every day: "Blessed art Thou, O Lord our God and God of our fathers, God of Abraham, God of Isaac, and God of Jacob. . . ." But in a little while we add:

"Remember us for life, O King who delights in life; inscribe us in the Book of Life, for Thy sake, O God of life."

The Jewish New Year

The word *life* is used four times in that one short prayer. And Rosh Hashanah is about life. It has nothing to do with death although the season is autumn when nature begins to die. But Jews have faith in God as the God of life. We know that spring will come and life will renew itself.

The early Babylonians and Persians began their year in the spring when the world turned green again. The Romans began the custom of marking the new year in

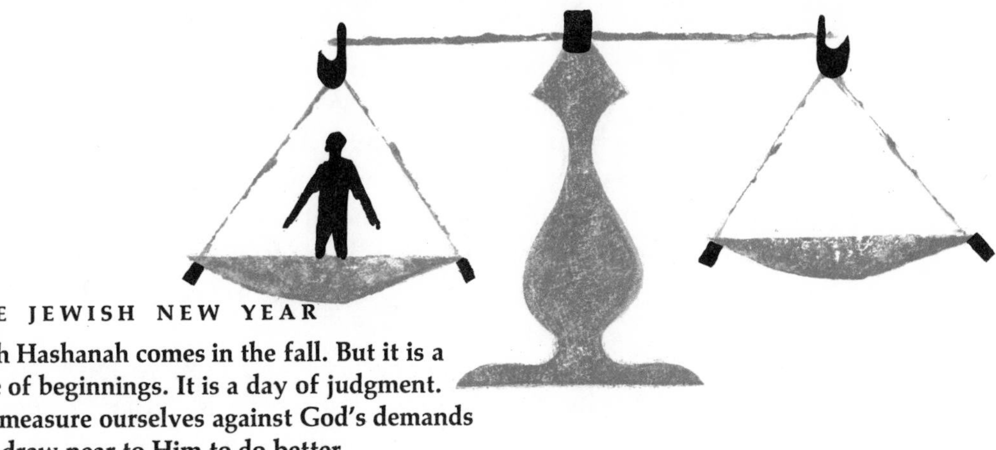

THE JEWISH NEW YEAR

Rosh Hashanah comes in the fall. But it is a time of beginnings. It is a day of judgment. We measure ourselves against God's demands and draw near to Him to do better.

the middle of winter. But the Hebrews chose to begin their year at the beginning of autumn, when nature is ripe and blossoming—and about to die.

It isn't only the season that makes the Jewish New Year different from that of other peoples. For most of the people, the New Year is celebrated as a time to let loose and do things you normally can't—or wouldn't. Today many people mark New Year's Eve with wild parties, the blowing of horns, too much drinking, and generally acting silly. The Jewish New Year has a quite different feeling. It is a time for quiet happiness, for serious thinking. It is a time for looking forward and for looking back.

Rosh Hashanah and Yom Kippur are different from other Jewish holidays because they do not mark any historical event. They simply begin the new year in the Jewish way. *Rosh* means "head" or "beginning," *shanah* means "year," so *Rosh Hashanah* means the beginning of the year. It is not the anniversary of a great battle, or a great man, or an important change in the history of the Jews. The traditional prayer book does say it is the anniversary of the day the earth was created. And creating a new year is a little like creating a new world.

If each day were like every other day, all time would soon become a dull blur. We wouldn't be able to recognize change or see growth from one time to another. That's one reason for making days into weeks, with a shining Shabbat at the end of each week. And that's one reason for marking the close of one year and the beginning of the next with a New Year's Day, Rosh Hashanah.

Starting anew

Man has to stop every now and then to look back to where he was, to check where he is, to look ahead to where he will be next week or next year. It's as if he sees himself every day in a kind of flat mirror that only shows the side facing the mirror. But on Rosh Hashanah, he steps back, and looks into a kind of three-sided mirror that shows all sides. By this new view, you can see if you are growing in the direction you wish to grow. And if not, you can make corrections.

That's why our Rabbis said: "God will say unto Israel, even to all humanity, 'My children, I look upon you as if today, Rosh Hashanah, you have been made for Me anew; as if today I created you, a new being, a new people, a new humanity.' " Rosh Hashanah is the day when we get another chance, when the New Year means a gift of new time in which to be good.

God's measure for man

Whenever we measure anything we must have a standard against which to measure. In measuring cloth it is a yardstick. In measuring land it is the surveyor's tape measure. In measuring a man, we do not use another man as a standard—no matter how good that other man might be. The right measurement of a man, according to Jewish belief, is God's image of man. We measure ourselves against what God wants us to be.

We do this measuring on Rosh Hashanah and the days that follow. We try to get as close to God as we can. When we are near Him we can feel that some things we did were very bad and others very good. We can tell God wants us to give up the bad, to do the good. We can sense what we should be doing with our lives. That is what we mean when we say God judges us and Rosh Hashanah is the Day of Judgment. On that day we ask what God wants of us. Are we getting closer or are we falling behind? What must we do in the new year to be closer to Him next Rosh Hashanah?

A Day of Remembering

If you read it very carefully, the Torah doesn't say the new year begins on the first day of Tishri. It does say that this is a holiday, a day of complete rest. And it does say that this is a Day of Remembering. That is the first meaning of our holiday.

We remember the year just ending, and the years before; we remember our own past, and our father's past, and our forefathers' back to the beginning of time.

The world changes each year, and man changes. Mountains are thrust up and mountains are worn away. What was sea is now dry land; what was dry land is now sea. What was forest is now desert, and where it was desert, green things now grow.

So it is with man. He grows from infancy to childhood to adult. He grows from ignorance to knowledge. He grows from generation to generation. How our grandfathers grew helps decide what we are; and how we grow will help decide what future generations will be.

The Day of Judging

We remember all this on the Day of Remembering—on Rosh Hashanah.

Rosh Hashanah is also called *Yom ha-Din,* the Day of Judging. On our New Year's day we come to be judged—by God. Have we grown enough inside? Have we grown straight or crooked? How close do we come to God's standard?

If you go to a court where men are judged by other men, the persons being judged are worried. Their faces are sad. They wear dark quiet clothes. They probably didn't eat before because their worry took away their appetite. But when a Jew stands before God to be judged on Rosh Hashanah, he is not sad. He is reflective. He wears his finest clothes. He eats a festival meal. He knows that God the Judge will do everything possible to say "Not guilty." God wants justice, but, particularly on Rosh Hashanah, He wants mercy more. He does not want to punish us but to get us to do the right. So He will give us another chance in a new year if we only show we care.

Some Jewish holidays are celebrated outside Israel for two days instead of one, or eight days instead of seven, because people were not sure of the calendar in ancient days. But Rosh Hashanah is celebrated for two days everywhere, even in Israel. According to the Palestinian Talmud, the Early Prophets ordered the two-day celebration because of the importance of this day. Reform Jews, however, usually observe only one day.

The Rosh Hashanah feast

At home, Rosh Hashanah eve begins as do all Jewish holidays—with the mother of the family lighting the candles with the regular holiday blessing:

וְצִוָּנוּ לְהַדְלִיק נֵר שֶׁל־יוֹם טוֹב:

and commanded us to light the holiday candles.

There will also be the holiday Kiddush and a Rosh Hashanah feast. Again there are two ḥallot on the table. We are told that they used to be baked in fancy shapes —a ladder or a bird or a crown. Today the holiday ḥallah is more likely to be round rather than long, and its top swirls up to a peak rather than being twisted.

After the ha-Motzi blessing, each person takes a piece of the ḥallah, dips it in honey, and on eating it, says, "May it be a sweet and good year." Sometimes

ROSH HASHANAH AT HOME

Rosh Hashanah eve is celebrated with the lighting of candles, a holiday blessing, the holiday Kiddush—and a special feast. Dipping ḥallah in honey we say, "May the new year be sweet."

apples dipped in honey are eaten for the same reason. The use of apples may have started this way. People thought it would be a nice idea to start the year with the Sheheḥeyanu blessing: "who has kept us alive and given us strength and made it possible for us to reach this happy day." So they would save a new fruit for eating for the first time that year on Rosh Hashanah. That is one of the times to say the Sheheḥeyanu. In many parts of Europe the apples were ripe about Rosh Hashanah time. So apples and honey were a good reason for saying the blessing and praying for a good year.

The sounding of the shofar

In addition to Day of Remembering and Day of Judging, there is another name for Rosh Hashanah: *Yom Teruah,* "Day of the Sounding of the Shofar." And the shofar is the main feature of the Rosh Hashanah morning service.

The shofar is usually the horn of a ram, a male sheep, but it can be the horn of any kosher animal except a cow or a calf. In ancient days, the shofar called the Jews to attention. It was what the bagpipes are to

SOUNDING OF THE SHOFAR

The Shofar is sounded severa times in the synagogue service except on the Sabbath. Specia prayers are recited, marking God's kingship, recalling wha we have done, and recounting the revelation at Sinai

the Scots and Irish, what the drum and bugle are to modern armies—and much more. The ancient Jews sounded the shofar to announce the coming of the new moon, to lead their armies into battle, to announce the coming of the king, and as a call to assembly. In a sense, we still use it as a symbol of new moon, battle, and king. Today the sounding of the shofar announces the new moon that begins the new year. It calls us to the continuing battle of Israel to bring about the Days of the Messiah, the world of peace and justice. It asks us to be loyal to the One King over all the universe.

The Talmud says that when the Jews sound the shofar on Rosh Hashanah, God gets up from His throne of justice and sits down on His throne of mercy. He knows they want another chance and He wants them to have it.

The shofar is sounded several times during the morning service of Rosh Hashanah—except on Shabbat when it is not sounded at all.

The shofar prayers

The high point of the Rosh Hashanah service comes when the special shofar prayers are recited. There are three groups of them, each with its own idea, and after each the shofar is blown. The first group marks God's kingship over the universe. The second group is for remembrance of what we have done. The third group is about what the shofar has always meant to Jews; it reminds us of Mount Sinai where God and the Jews made their covenant. It makes us think of the coming of the Days of the Messiah. It brings to mind all the Jews who have listened, who are listening, and who will be listening to the great sound of the shofar.

Why do we still sound the shofar—that difficult, sometimes harsh-sounding, horn—rather than some clear, sweet, modern instrument? Well, why go to Washington to walk where Lincoln walked, to Philadelphia to be in the same room where the Declaration of Independence was signed, to Masada in Israel to stand where the Jews defied Rome's mightiest legions? We sound the shofar because that very same instrument, in that very same shape and material, called Jews to assembly, to battle, to God, from our earliest days. When we hear it, we remember. And no modern instruments can do that for us. It's not the sound that counts. It's not being pretty we care about. It's being part of our people, close to God. There's no sound that we hear during the whole year like the sound of the shofar. So it's very special.

There are three different kinds of blasts sounded on the shofar: *tekiah, shevarim,* and *teruah. Tekiah* is a short note followed by a long higher one. *Shevarim* is three more speedy *tekiot*. *Teruah* is a series of very fast notes, nine or twelve of them, followed by the tekiah note. It is not easy to describe the sounds with words. You have to hear them.

Bowing before God

Another part of the Rosh Hashanah service is different from all other services in the synagogue and outside. On Rosh Hashanah, and only on Rosh Hashanah and Yom Kippur, Jews bow low to the ground as part of the service.

Since the days of the Temple, Jews have not got down on their knees or stretched out flat before God except on these two holidays. On Rosh Hashanah and Yom Kippur Jews make a special point of accepting God as king over all. Then, in traditional Ashkenazi synagogues, Jews not only kneel, they fall on their face before God. It is done as the cantor recites the words of the *Alénu* prayer:

וַאֲנַחְנוּ כֹּרְעִים וּמִשְׁתַּחֲוִים וּמוֹדִים לִפְנֵי מֶלֶךְ מַלְכֵי הַמְּלָכִים
הַקָּדוֹשׁ בָּרוּךְ הוּא: שֶׁהוּא נוֹטֶה שָׁמַיִם וְיֹסֵד אָרֶץ. וּמוֹשַׁב
יְקָרוֹ בַּשָּׁמַיִם מִמַּעַל. וּשְׁכִינַת עֻזּוֹ בְּגָבְהֵי מְרוֹמִים:

We bend the knee and prostrate ourselves and make acknowledgment before the King of Kings, the Holy One, blessed be He, who stretched out the heavens and laid the foundations of the earth, whose glorious throne is in the heavens and the home of whose majesty is in the loftiest heights.

While the cantor recites this he and some of the men in the congregation will stretch out on the floor to show their obedience and faith in God, the King. (This is not done in Sephardic or in most Reform synagogues.)

Rosh Hashanah customs

After the service—the evening before as well as in the morning—there is a special Rosh Hashanah greeting. Instead of *Ḥag Sameaḥ* or *Gut Yom Tov*, the usual holiday greetings, we say *Leshanah Tovah Tikatevu*, "May God write you down for a good year [in the Book of Life]." That is the greeting you will find in Hebrew on most Jewish New Year cards.

Another Rosh Hashanah custom, *Tashlich*, is only about five hundred years old. On the afternoon of the first day of Rosh Hashanah traditional Jews go to the nearest river and empty the dust in their pockets into the water. Some say this was done to show that man can shake himself loose from sin and correct his ways. Others think it is connected with the verses from the prophet Micah, recited during the ceremony. It says:

God will have compassion on us;
He will tread our iniquities under foot;
*You will throw [*tashlich, *in Hebrew] all their sins into the depths of the sea.*
You will keep faith with Jacob, and mercy with Abraham,
As you promised our fathers long ago.

This custom may have come to the Jews from other people. But the Jews gave it a special meaning, just as they gave the whole idea of the New Year a special meaning.

GOALS FOR THE NEW YEAR

The Jew looks forward with faith to a better future, a future of peace and tranquillity when, as Isaiah says, ". . . the wolf shall dwell with the lamb . . . the calf and the young lion together . . ."

For us, the New Year does not mean trying hard to forget what we did wrong last year. We do not celebrate the end of the old year so wildly that we cannot remember what went before. On Rosh Hashanah, the Jew stands before God to be judged. His past is measured. The time he spent doing good is weighed against the time he spent in sin, the evil he has caused. When he feels that, and makes up his mind to change, he knows God will help him as he tries to face the new year with faith and confidence. Now his past, and the past of all his people, will help shape this future. And making the coming year a better one, he will help his people bring the Days of the Messiah a little closer.

22
Yom Kippur

The day of forgiveness

Like other Jewish holidays, Yom Kippur has several names and descriptions. But more than anything else, Yom Kippur is the day of forgiveness. On that day we forgive and are forgiven.

Forgiveness is a necessary part of growing. If we do not forgive others for the wrongs and hurts they did us, then our pain turns to hate. And just as love is life, so hate is a kind of death. If we hate, a part of us dies. With part of us dead, we cannot grow properly. We grow crookedly, misshapen by hate.

So we must learn to ask others to forgive us; and we must learn to forgive others. This is not easy. It is very hard to ask someone to forgive you for the wrong you have done him. It is even harder to forgive someone who has wronged you. But if they mean what they say, if they honestly seek forgiveness, Judaism says that you must give it. If not, the world would soon fill with

NEED FOR ATONEMENT

Yom Kippur is a day of atonement, of asking forgiveness for sin. Jews value forgiveness. They ask God and their fellow man to forgive them, if need be. They grant forgiveness to others.

hate and we would all die. The Talmud says that he who forgives those who have wronged him has his own sins forgiven by God. The Jews have always believed that forgiveness is one of God's greatest gifts to man.

Though the Jewish people often sinned in serving God, they knew that He would have patience with them in carrying out His laws. God keeps giving the Jews another chance, another year, another opportunity to follow His way. And the Jews try to do better every year. They don't always succeed; they have failed to do better almost as often as they have succeeded. But they tried and they keep trying. The greatest mitzvah is to try to follow the mitzvot. That's one explanation of why the Jews have been able to live for so many thousands of years.

The Temple service

After the Second Temple had been built, Yom Kippur was clearly the holiest single day of the Jewish year. It was called the Great Day, or merely the Day. By the time the Second Temple was destroyed in 70 C.E., many Jews were no longer going to the synagogue or the Temple every day. They were no longer as careful as they should have been about sacrifices. Nevertheless on Yom Kippur they still fasted and attended services.

The most important services took place in the Temple. The High Priest showed himself in his gold robes to the people every Shabbat but he did not perform the daily or weekly services. He left those to the other priests. But on Yom Kippur he himself conducted the ceremonies. He put on linen robes instead of gold and before God he confessed his own sins and the sins of all Israel.

He did something else quite special. A Jew does not say the Name of God. Although this Name is written in the Bible, we do not read it as written but say instead *Adonai,* my Lord. The same in our prayers. But on Yom Kippur in the days of the Temple the High Priest actually said God's Name, as it is written, ten times. And as he said it, the priests and the entire congregation would fall to the ground and say, "Blessed be the Name, the glory of His kingdom is forever and ever." (We say that after the Shema to this day.)

Temple sacrifices

The Torah commands special sacrifices for Yom Kippur. Two goats, exactly alike, were brought to the altar. The High Priest put his hand into a jug in which were two tablets of clay; one was marked, "for God," the other, "for Azazel" (the evil one). The High Priest would pull a tablet out of the jug and place it on the head of one goat, then the other tablet on the head of the other goat. A red sash was tied around the horns of the goat chosen for Azazel. The High Priest said a prayer admitting all the sins the Jews had done, and then the Azazel goat was driven into the wilderness. There he was run off a cliff. It was as if he carried the sins of the people with him. That is why we still speak of a "scapegoat," one who carries the sins of others.

The other goat was sacrificed to God in the usual way.

After the destruction of the Temple and the end of the High Priests, Jews did not have someone to confess their sins for them. Nor were there any more sacrifices. They confessed their own sins and they had a good substitute for sacrifice—repentance, prayer and charity.

But the memory of the great Temple service never

ATONEMENT THEN AND NOW

In the time of the Second Temple the High Priest confessed his sins and those of Israel, and himself performed the service on Yom Kippur. A goat was driven into the wilderness, bearing the sins of Israel. A second goat was sacrificed to God. Since the fall of the Temple each Jew seeks his own atonement with God. For sacrifice he offers repentance, prayer and charity. In the synagogue the entire congregation offers prayers of confession.

died. We still read about and remember it in our Yom Kippur services in the synagogue.

Atonement today

In the two thousand years since the last Temple service, the Yom Kippur service has changed its place and its ways, but not its meaning. Each Jew must still get rid of his own wrongdoing—and only he knows what wrongs he committed last year.

But it is not enough for each individual Jew to cleanse himself of sin on Yom Kippur. The High Priest, remember, spoke for all the Jews. The Jewish community must be rid of its burden of sin. We are supposed to follow God's laws as a Jewish community, helping and loving one another. Sometimes we are good. We give to charity, build Jewish schools, defend our Jewish brothers who are attacked, work to build a better society for everyone. But we do not get together to do all the things we should do. So on Yom Kippur, the whole family of Jews comes before God to make up for its failures.

יוֹם כִּפּוּר

We translate *Yom Kippur* to mean "Day of Atonement." But *kippur* also means "getting rid of," so *Yom Kippur* really means "The Day of Getting Rid of Our Sins." *Atonement* means to be loving once again. When we sin it is as if we and God became strangers. When we try to make up for our sins, it is as if we became friends again. That is atonement. Someone once pointed out that atonement is spelled as if it said at-one-ment, as if we were, again, at one with God.

When a Jew takes part in the Yom Kippur service in his synagogue, he does so not only to make atonement for his personal sins but to take part in a community affair. He goes to be part of the entire congregation of Israel coming to atone to God for not having fulfilled their part of the covenant.

Even those Jews who do not attend services throughout the year generally attend Yom Kippur services. Our Rabbis gave a simple explanation of why it is good to pray together rather than separately. They said that two men can carry a load farther than one man, and ten men can carry it still farther. So if all the people pray together, it is easier to carry whatever load of sin they have.

Fasting and repenting

When we fast on Tisha be-Av, we do so in sorrow for the loss of the Temple. But when we fast on Yom Kippur, we do not do so in sorrow. On Yom Kippur, our minds must be free of all thoughts except those of repentance for the wrongs we did during the year, and of the better life we will live next year. We do not want to give time to eating. It will take us away from the more important Yom Kippur thoughts. And the slight pain of hunger helps us remember how human we are, how much we depend on God. Eating is so much a part of the celebration of our holidays—the Seder on Pesaḥ, hamantaschen on Purim, the meals in the sukkah on Sukkot. It has a big part in our social life; visiting relatives and friends is almost always marked by eating. On Yom Kippur we turn this around. We give up all food, as a symbol of our interest only in repentance. This will be the only day when we stay at synagogue from morning until sundown. A whole day, every part of it, is set aside to make atonement.

We do not fast on Yom Kippur for God. He gets nothing out of it. Nor do we fast for others to see how pious we are. We fast for ourselves. But some people are too young to fast, some too old, some too sick, for some it would be a punishment rather than a privilege. In any case, no holiday or ritual is as important as life to a Jew. That's why, on the day of the great fast, those who would suffer from fasting are not asked to fast.

Regard for life

A Ḥasidic rabbi was once asked why he was so easygoing when it came to allowing people to eat on Yom Kippur. He said, "It is not that I am so easygoing when it comes to fasting, but that I am so strict when it comes to the commandment to save life."

And, of course, the comfort and safety of animals must not be endangered by Yom Kippur or any other holiday. They must be fed and cared for.

Once the great Rabbi Israel Salanter, who lived about a hundred years ago, was walking to the synagogue on the eve of Yom Kippur. On his way he saw a cow that belonged to a non-Jew lost and caught in some bushes. Rabbi Israel freed the animal and walked it to its barn. Meanwhile the sun went down and the congregation was waiting in the synagogue to begin the Yom Kippur eve services. When the rabbi did not appear, the leaders of the congregation went to look for him. They thought that only a great misfortune could keep the rabbi from Kol Nidre. When the men of the congregation found Rabbi Israel, he was feeding the cow in its stall. As he said, the mitzvah of saving life is greater than the mitzvah of observing Yom Kippur.

Yom Kippur eve

The fast of Yom Kippur starts as the sun goes down. It should not start earlier because that would be painful. That's why there are rules about the last meal before sundown. It can't be too little because that would make it less than a meal. And it can't be too much because a heavy meal makes us sleepy and we need to be wide awake during the evening service.

Once again there are candles. Only the commandment blessing ends:

וְצִוָּנוּ לְהַדְלִיק נֵר שֶׁל־יוֹם הַכִּפֻּרִים:

and commanded us to light the Yom Kippur candles.

And since the day itself is a fast there is no Kiddush, there is no Motzi. However, some people used to put a fine cloth over the dining room table and spread books on the cloth. This showed that Yom Kippur was celebrated in that house, not with food on the table, but with Torah and prayer and study.

The family goes to the synagogue for the Yom Kippur services. In the old days, and in some places today, Jews did not wear shoes inside the synagogue on Yom Kippur. Perhaps that was a special way of showing how sorry people were. Others say that when all Israel repents its sins the whole world becomes holy. And we do not want to step on holy ground with our shoes. So we take them off.

YOM KIPPUR EVE

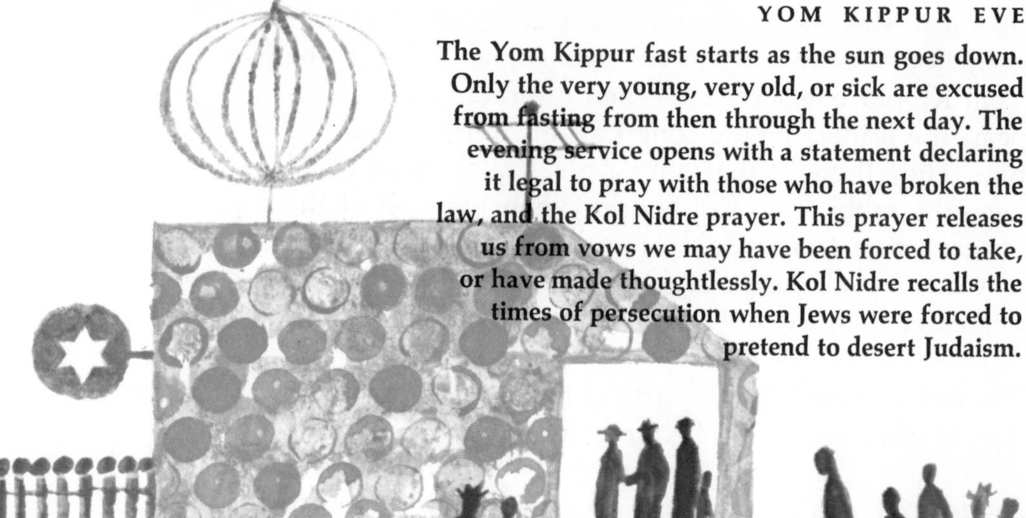

The Yom Kippur fast starts as the sun goes down. Only the very young, very old, or sick are excused from fasting from then through the next day. The evening service opens with a statement declaring it legal to pray with those who have broken the law, and the Kol Nidre prayer. This prayer releases us from vows we may have been forced to take, or have made thoughtlessly. Kol Nidre recalls the times of persecution when Jews were forced to pretend to desert Judaism.

Kol Nidre No prayer comes from so deep within the Jewish soul, few prayers bring tears so easily to the eyes, as does the opening prayer of Yom Kippur—the *Kol Nidre.* This feeling for Kol Nidre does not come so much from the words of this prayer but from its beautiful melody. As we hear those notes memories rise up in the mind and the heart—for the heart remembers, too. In a way, Kol Nidre is much of Jewish history for the last two thousand years; Kol Nidre is a hymn to the faith of a hundred generations of Jews who refused to stop being Jews, who knew that as the Jews served God they were doing the best thing any man can do.

So the Yom Kippur eve service is often called the Kol Nidre service. It begins with the cantor or rabbi going before the Ark. Two men stand with him, one on each side, all three holding Scrolls of the Torah, and face the congregation. The official opening of the service is this unusual sentence:

By authority of the Court in Heaven, and of the Court of men here on earth, with the permission of God and with the permission of this holy congregation, we declare it to be lawful to pray together with those who have transgressed.

Then the cantor sings the Kol Nidre:

All vows, bonds, promises, obligations, and oaths with which we have vowed, sworn, and bound ourselves from this Day of Atonement unto the next Day of Atonement [or from the last Day of Atonement to this] of all these, we repent. Let them be absolved, released, annulled, made void, and of no effect; they shall not be binding, nor shall they have any power. Our vows shall not be vows; our bonds shall not be bonds; and our oaths shall not be oaths.

Forced or thoughtless vows

Kol Nidre has nothing to do with the oaths that a Jew swears in court, or the bonds or contracts he signs in business. Kol Nidre releases a Jew only from vows he made to God—and then only if he was in fear of his life or because he was not thinking. The vows that the Kol Nidre prayer asks God to wipe out are only the vows between man and God.

For example, although the Kol Nidre prayer is over a thousand years old, it is always associated with the Spanish Jews of the fourteenth and fifteenth centuries. In those dark days, many Jews were given the choice of death or conversion to Christianity. Many Jews died. Others accepted Christianity—out loud. But in their hearts they remained Jews. As they accepted Christianity under threat of death by torture, they cried out—silently—"I do this because I am forced."

Ordinarily, these Jews, having publicly accepted another religion, would not be allowed to pray with the congregation of Israel. They had transgressed; they had sinned; they had broken the commandments. But many of them, although they were burned to death if caught, remained secret Jews. On Yom Kippur eve, the secret Jews would come to pray together with the open Jews. But first the congregation declared that it was right to pray together with those who had transgressed; that the vows they had made to another god were not vows; that the oaths they gave were not binding.

There are other vows which we make without thinking: A father, watching his very ill child struggling for life, may swear, "God, if you allow my child to live, I will give everything I own to charity." But if he kept this vow, his family would be beggared; the child he is trying to save would go hungry. So this vow is wiped out with the Kol Nidre prayer. Someone else, in deep anger, might say, "I hope God strikes this man dead." Such oaths, too, are made nothing by Kol Nidre.

But all the regular vows a person makes in his lifetime—pledges in business, oaths in court, marriage vows, many more—are not affected by Kol Nidre.

Prayers of confession

After the Kol Nidre, the regular evening service continues with many special Yom Kippur prayers. Among them are the confession of sins—the *Viddui.*

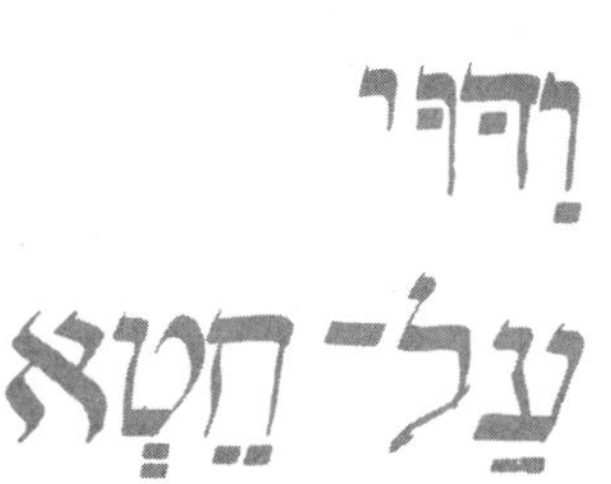

The most famous is the long confession, called the *Al Ḥet.* It has two sentences about our sins for each letter of the alphabet. It goes this way:

For the sin which we have done because we were forced to or because we wanted to,
For the sin which we have done by hardening our hearts.
For the sin which we have done unknowingly, . . .
For the sin which we have done by wronging our neighbor, . . .
For the sin which we have done by turning away from our parents and teachers, . . .
For all these, O God of forgiveness, forgive us, pardon us, grant us atonement.

CONFESSING TOGETHER

In the synagogue prayers of confession, the entire congregation joins in confessing sins of which many individuals are innocent. They do so—saying "we," not "I"—because we are all bound together. We are all responsible for the need, grief, ignorance that may cause people to sin.

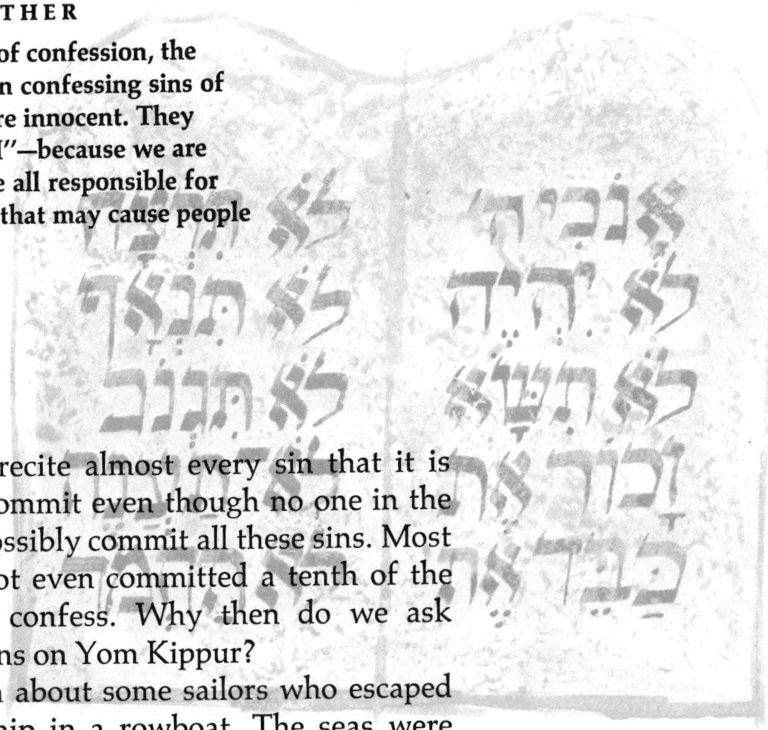

In the Al Ḥet we recite almost every sin that it is possible for man to commit even though no one in the congregation could possibly commit all these sins. Most of the people have not even committed a tenth of the sins they each now confess. Why then do we ask pardon for all these sins on Yom Kippur?

There is a Midrash about some sailors who escaped from their sinking ship in a rowboat. The seas were stormy and the little boat began to take in water. One of the sailors began to dig a hole under his seat to let out the water. The other sailors jumped on him and took away his knife. "Why do you stop me?" he cried. "I was digging a hole under my seat, not yours."

So it is with sin. Sin corrupts not only the person who commits it, but the entire community. And very few men commit sins because they are mean or evil. Sins are committed out of fear, ignorance, hunger, loneliness, revenge or anger. So, though we may not have sinned ourselves, we have caused others to sin by denying them food, by making them despair, by hurting them. We share their sin. Only in a perfect world, where there is no hunger and no war, when justice is every man's portion, can we say, "I have not sinned."

That is why, too, when we recite the great Al Ḥet, we say, "For the sin which *we* have committed . . ." Not "I" have committed, but "we" have committed. We do not ask pardon only for ourselves; we ask pardon for all our people and the world.

The great Rabbi Isaac Luria, who lived in the sixteenth century, explained: "Israel is a body and every Jew is a limb of that body. That is why we are responsible for one another when we sin."

The symphony of the service

The Yom Kippur service is like a great piece of music, a symphony. There are different movements or parts, each played separately, then combined, until they all come together in a great burst of music and feeling. The great opening chord is the Kol Nidre, then it quiets down a bit, crashing out again with the Al Ḥet. So the service varies all day long.

Morning and afternoon services

By the time of the morning service on Yom Kippur Day, the Jew has already gone 12 or 14 hours without food. There is a slight pain of hunger but it does not bother him. Instead, it increases his feeling for the great symphony of the service; it increases his feeling of togetherness with all Israel.

There are two Torah readings during the Yom Kippur services, morning and afternoon. But both times it is the Haftarah, the reading from the Prophets, which most people love. The morning Haftarah is from the prophet Isaiah. He says: It is not enough to fast. You do not atone simply by fasting. Only by doing something for your fellow man can you overcome the sins of man. In the middle of the fast of Yom Kippur we are told what a true fast would be:

Is not this the fast that I have chosen?
To loosen the ties of wickedness,
To undo the ropes of the yoke,

And to let the oppressed go free,
And that you break every yoke?
Is it not to give bread to the hungry,
And that you bring the homeless into your house?
When you see the naked, to clothe him,
And not to hide yourself from your fellow man?

Memorial prayers

After the Haftarah reading in the morning service there are memorial prayers—*Yizkor*—for the dead. Not only the dead of the congregation, but all the Jews dead of persecution and oppression. On Yom Kippur, the end of the Days of Awe, we die in a way, and are reborn again as we shed our sins and start the year afresh. So it is time to think of those who went before us. In most synagogues the Yom Kippur Yizkor services now include prayers for the six million Jews who died under the Nazis.

The service reaches another high point in the afternoon when the *Avodah* is read. This describes the Yom Kippur service in the Temple in Jerusalem.

The story of Jonah

Then comes the afternoon Torah reading and its great Haftarah. Most Haftarot are rather small parts of one of the books of the Prophets. The Haftarah for the afternoon service of Yom Kippur is different; it is the entire Book of Jonah. There are two main points in this

DAY OF YOM KIPPUR

The Book of Jonah is read on Yom Kippur to show the need for obedience to God's word, and that God's mercy is given to all—even idol worshipers—who repent of wrongdoing.

book—and neither has anything to do with a whale. God commands Jonah to go to the city of Nineveh. But Jonah tries to run away from God. (That's why he took the ship and wound up in the fish.) Eventually he gets to Nineveh. The people there were very wicked and Jonah must have thought they deserved to be punished. Besides they were great enemies of the Jews. So why should Jonah go to speak to them? But the Ninevites listened to Jonah. They repented and changed their ways. The entire city with its whole population was saved from destruction. Jonah didn't like it but God did.

What the Book of Jonah says is—

Man cannot escape God, no matter where he flees. Nor can man escape the responsibilities that are his because he is a man. You must face God and you must face your duties as a human being.

God's mercy is over all the world, over Jew and non-Jew, over those who believe in God and those who worship idols. All that is necessary is to recognize wrongdoing and try to correct it. The people of Nineveh were idol-worshipers, but because they repented their sins, God was good to them.

Close of the service

As the sun begins to set, the great symphony of Yom Kippur slows down. The congregation becomes still, as if awaiting a great event. The Neilah service approaches. *Neilah* means "closing." The word originally applied to the gates of the Temple, which were closed every day at sundown. But this ordinary meaning was given a much deeper religious meaning. The closing of the Temple gates came to be the symbol of the closing of the gates of heaven to prayers of repentance, of the last chance to change the decree, the judgment written in the books of heaven. From Rosh Hashanah to this point the congregation has prayed: "Inscribe us in the

THE CLOSING OF THE DAY OF FAST

The Neilah service closes Yom Kippur with the cry, "Adonai Hu ha-Elohim—The Lord, He is God," and a blast of the shofar. Freed from sin by repentance, and sealed in the Book of Life, the worshipers turn from past to future.

Book of Life." Now the prayer changes to: "Seal us in the Book of Life." The Days of Awe, the Ten Days of Repentance, are coming to an end.

There are three great Jewish statements: the Shema; the blessing of God's Name; and the cry, *Adonai Hu ha-Elohim*—"the Lord, He is God." Each year they are said at the end of the Neilah service. The congregation declares for everyone to hear that Adonai is the only God, that they will serve Him, that they will spend all the years He gives them following His Law. As the last great cry echoes in all the synagogues in all the world, a long blast is blown on the shofar, and the fast of Yom Kippur is over.

This great day, begun in tears, spent in hunger, closed with a great shout, is solemn—but not unhappy. It is, as a matter of fact, a very hopeful holiday. It could even be considered a happy day because in a sense we are renewed this day; time begins again. The old year in which we made mistakes, caused errors, did wrong, is closed. And if we repented honestly and completely, we are free of the sins of the past year. The past is less important; the future is more important.

The goal of time

What does it all add up to,
The days and weeks, the months and years?
Where are we going?
What does it mean?

We Jews have a dream.
A vision of a world much like ours—but different.
A world of love, of justice, of understanding;
A world of plenty and of peace;
A world where men are not afraid of each other
But are true to God—
And to one another.

This dream has been with us for four thousand years;
It has given us strength and hope,
Helped us build good communities and loving families,
Kept us working for good when other men despaired.

That is the meaning of our lives—
Measured by the ordinary days and the holidays.
We spend our days and weeks, months and years,
Helping bring God's Kingdom in the Days of the
Messiah.

23

The End of Days

Toward a better world

Hope is a part of growing up—for individuals, for a people, for a nation. If we do not dream of the future, make plans for the future, and have some faith that they can come true, we will remain forever children. Without hope we would have no courage to try to be more than we are.

The Jews, from their earliest days, have had faith in the future. They were the first people to understand that time does not just keep repeating itself senselessly. Time has a goal and life has a purpose. History is a very long road that goes somewhere; it is not a circle that keeps coming back to its starting place.

Jews believe that the long road of history, the long succession of days, goes from somewhere less good to somewhere much better. There are detours on the road, rough places, places so dark you cannot see whether

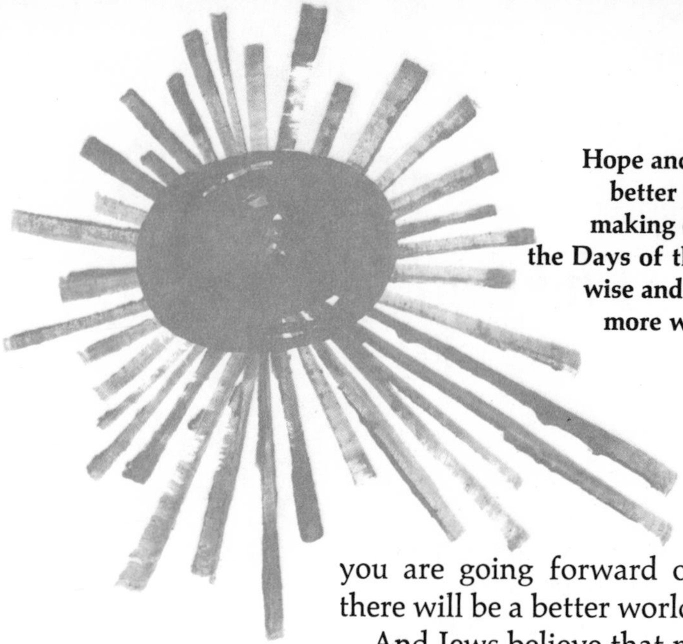

HOPE AND FAITH

Hope and faith in the future help us become better people. They help us do our part in making our world better, in bringing closer the Days of the Messiah when men will be free, wise and law-abiding, when there will be no more wars, when men will live together in justice and harmony.

you are going forward or backward. But in the end there will be a better world.

And Jews believe that man cannot be just a thoughtless traveler on this road of days. Men must try to straighten the road, lighten the dark places, smooth the rough spots. Men must try to hurry the world along toward the end of the journey of time, when the world will be a place of goodness, of justice, of peace, the time the prophets called "the End of Days."

Maimonides described the Days of the Messiah as a time when there will be no more oppression to keep people from fulfilling all the commandments; a time when wisdom will increase, when war will end, when there will be harmony among men, and when all worry and anxiety will be over. He said:

Let no one think that in the days of the Messiah any of the laws of nature will be set aside, or any new things be introduced into creation. The world will follow its normal course. . . . Israel will live securely among the wicked of the heathens who . . . will all accept the true religion, and will neither plunder nor destroy, and together with Israel earn a comfortable living in a legitimate way.

There was more to say but that was as much as Maimonides thought one could say clearly.

A calendar of years

Most calendars are for one year, each year being pretty much like every other year. But not the Jewish years. To keep reminding us that our years should add up to something good, the Torah has a special calendar of years. There are laws in the Torah that make some years quite different from others, teaching us of the great goal of history.

The Children of Israel, the Torah commands, shall celebrate every seventh year as a Sabbatical year—and every fiftieth year as a Jubilee year. *Sabbatical* means "Sabbath-like," and the Sabbatical year is a Sabbath for the land itself. During that year the earth was not touched by plow or harrow or hoe. Nothing was planted and the people ate what had been put aside from crops in the previous years. So every seventh year was a year of special trust in God, of faith that He would provide.

The Jubilee year was a kind of renewal, a kind of starting over again, perhaps a kind of revolution. When the twelve tribes settled in the Land of Israel, each tribe received an area for itself, and each family was given its own land to farm and on which to pasture their flocks. As the years passed, some families got poorer and some richer. Some families had to sell their land. But the sale of land was not forever. On the Jubilee year, every family returned to its own land and took possession of it again. Today we talk about giving land to the poor, of redistributing the land, as one way of wiping out poverty in poor countries. The Jubilee year was to do this for the Jews thousands of years ago.

The Jubilee year is supposed to begin on Yom Kippur when we are to "proclaim liberty throughout the land to all the inhabitants thereof." This verse from the Torah is on the Liberty Bell and the word *jubilee* has come to mean a great and joyous celebration.

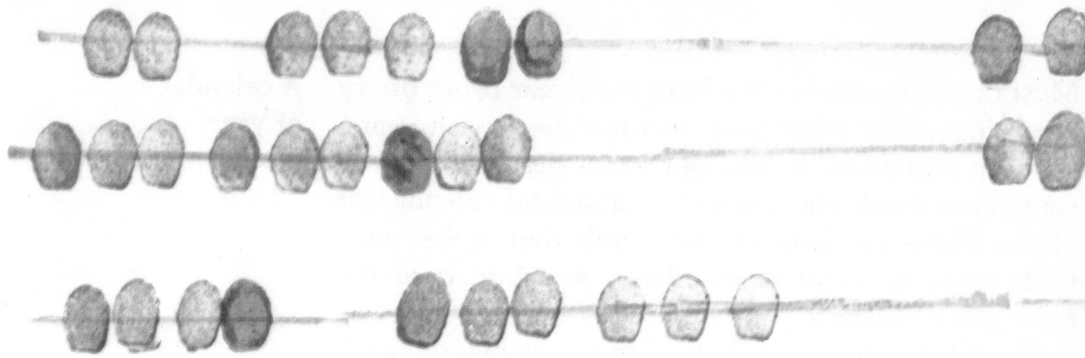

The Bible does not tell us of any occasion when the Jubilee year was observed. We do know from the Rabbis of later times that the Sabbatical year was kept in ancient Israel. Today, Orthodox Jewish farmers in Israel still observe it. The laws commanding it apply only to farming in Israel but the idea of the Sabbatical and Jubilee years serves as a reminder to Jews all over the world that not only our weeks and our months, but our years, too, ought to build a world of love and justice.

Hope for the End of Days

Throughout their very long journey on this road of days, many extraordinary things happened to and among our people. Perhaps the most extraordinary is that even though they suffered much from what other people did to them, they did not despair about people. They did not lose hope. They did not forget their dream of the End of Days. Every time they fulfilled a mitzvah on an ordinary day, they repeated their dream. Every Shabbat and every holiday was an expression of this hope. They could hold on to their hopes and dreams because they knew that they were not alone in their work of lighting the way. They knew that God, too, was working to bring all mankind to the End of Days.

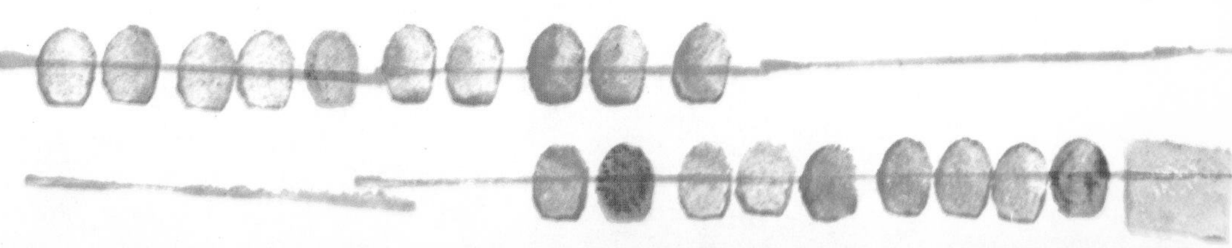

So God and the Jews, working together in history along with all other men of good will, try to move the world along toward the greatest of all holidays: the End of Days. We may not live to see that great day just as we may not accomplish all the things we hope for and all the things we dream of. But we try to do our part. Each mitzvah, each act of kindness and justice, moves us and our people an inch, a foot, a mile—in complete faith that God and man together will someday reach that goal of history.

In that time every day will be Pesaḥ because every day will be a day of freedom. Every day will be Rosh Hashanah because every day will begin a new year. Every day will be Yom Kippur because every day will be without sin. Every day will be Ḥanukkah because every day will be a day of miracles. Until then our calendar keeps us from forgetting, and the ceremonies of our lives keep us true.

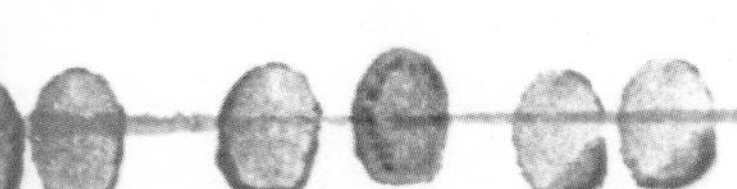

THE DAYS OF THE MESSIAH

The Jewish hope for the End of Days is expressed in each mitzvah, Sabbath, and holiday. The Jews are partners with God—along with all other men of good will—in helping the world toward the Days of the Messiah when man will be truly the image of God.

And what is your place in this great, long, crowded journey of the Jewish people? As a part of that people you are helping the world reach toward the End of Days. If you do not do your part no one can do it for you. But you can cover part of the journey; you can do part of the job—the more you do, the better. And God will see to it that we will eventually reach our goal.

That will be the End of Days, the Days of the Messiah. That will be the day when man will truly be the image of God. That will be the end of the journey for us all because the Jews will have accomplished what they set out to do.

Glossary of Hebrew terms

Afikoman, one half of the middle of the three matzot set before the father of the house at the Seder and saved to be eaten at the close of the Seder. See **Seder.** אֲפִיקוֹמָן

Bar Mitzvah, "son of the commandment," the mark of a boy's growth into young manhood at the age of thirteen. On reaching Bar Mitzvah age, a boy becomes responsible for his own deeds. בַּר מִצְוָה

Bat Mitzvah, "daughter of the commandment," representing for girls what Bar Mitzvah is for boys. בַּת מִצְוָה

Berit Milah, the name given the ceremony of circumcision. *Berit* means covenant; *milah* means circumcision. בְּרִית מִילָה

Besamim, spices, with reference to those used in the spice box for the *Havdalah* ceremony. See **Havdalah.** בְּשָׂמִים

Dayenu, "It would have been enough," is the name of a song-prayer sung during the Seder, thanking God for the wonders of the Exodus. דַּיֵּנוּ

Eshet Ḥayil, "woman of valor," refers to a poem in the Book of Proverbs. The father of the house recites this poem on Shabbat eve in honor of his wife. אֵשֶׁת־חַיִל

Etrog, a citrus fruit, the citron, carried with the *Lulav* during the ceremonies of Sukkot. See **Lulav; Sukkot.** אֶתְרוֹג

Etz Ḥayyim, the tree of life. This phrase is also used to describe the rollers on which the Torah is wound. עֵץ חַיִּים

Haftarah, the portion from one of the books of the Prophets read in the synagogue after the reading of the Torah portion. הַפְטָרָה

Haggadah, the story of Pesaḥ read and retold during the Seder. הַגָּדָה

Ha-Gomel, the blessing said after danger or serious illness has passed. הַגּוֹמֵל

Ḥag Sameaḥ, the festival greeting, which means "happy holiday." חַג שָׂמֵחַ

Hakkafot, parades around the synagogue led by men and boys carrying the Scrolls of the Torah. הַקָּפוֹת

Ḥallah, the braided Shabbat loaf of bread. חַלָּה

Ḥametz, any of the foods not permitted during Pesaḥ. See **Pesaḥ.** חָמֵץ

Ḥanukkah, the holiday celebrating the retaking of the Temple from the Syrians, and its cleansing. חֲנֻכָּה

Havdalah, the ceremony at the close of the Shabbat, marking the end of the holy day and the beginning of the every-days. הַבְדָּלָה

Ḥevrah Kaddisha, "holy brotherhood," referring to the society or committee of Jews who performed the mitzvah of watching over and arranging the dead for burial. חֶבְרָה קַדִּישָׁא

Hoshana Rabbah, the seventh day of Sukkot. See **Sukkot.** הוֹשַׁעְנָא רַבָּא

Kaddish, a basic Jewish prayer. In one form, the one most people know, it is the prayer said for the dead. קַדִּישׁ

Kashrut, the system of laws about what a Jew may and may not eat. כַּשְׁרוּת

כְּתוּבָּה **Ketubah,** the marriage contract, a paper signed by the bride and the bridegroom, two witnesses, and the rabbi, setting forth the fact of the marriage and the conditions of the marriage.

קִדּוּשׁ **Kiddush,** the blessing sanctifying the Sabbath or a festival, usually said over wine.

קִדּוּשִׁין **Kiddushin,** a form of the word "holy," referring to the marriage ceremony, because marriage makes holy the sharing of two people's lives.

כָּל־נִדְרֵי **Kol Nidre,** the opening prayer of the Yom Kippur eve service.

לַ״ג בָּעוֹמֶר **Lag ba-Omer,** a holiday on the 33rd day of the days of the Omer, the 33rd day that a sheaf of barley was brought to the Temple. See **Omer.**

לְשָׁנָה טוֹבָה תִּכָּתֵבוּ **Leshanah Tovah Tikatevu,** the Rosh Hashanah greeting. It means "may God write you down for a good life (in the year ahead)."

לוּלָב **Lulav,** palm branch, refers to the branches of palm, myrtle and willow tied together and used in the ceremonies of the Sukkot holiday.

מַעֲרִיב **Ma'ariv,** evening, refers to the evening service.

מָעוֹת חִטִּים **Maot Ḥittim,** "wheat-money," refers to the money given to the poor to buy matzah and other necessities for Pesaḥ.

מַצֵּבָה **Matzevah,** the monument or headstone put over a grave.

מְגִלָּה **Megillah,** scroll, refers to the five books of the Bible that are often written on separate small scrolls. These include Esther, Song of Songs, Ruth, Lamentations and Ecclesiastes. The *Megillah* of the Book of Esther (generally referred to as "the Megillah") is read on Purim.

מְנוֹרָה **Menorah,** the seven-branched candlestick. The Ḥanukkah menorah has branches for nine candles.

מְזוּזָה **Mezuzah,** a box, usually of metal or ceramic, holding a parchment on which is written the beginning verses of the *Shema*. The *Mezuzah* is nailed to the doorpost of a Jewish home. See **Shema.**

מִנְחָה **Minḥah,** afternoon, refers to the afternoon service.

מִצְוָה **Mitzvah,** commandment, a law of God. To do a mitzvah is to do what God asks of us; to do a good or kind deed.

מִזְרָח **Mizraḥ,** "east." For Jews living in Europe, North Africa and the Americas it is the direction of Jerusalem.

נְעִילָה **Neilah,** "closing," the closing prayer and service of Yom Kippur.

נֵר תָּמִיד **Ner Tamid,** Eternal Light, refers to the light kept perpetually burning over the Ark in the synagogue.

עוֹמֶר **Omer,** "sheaf," or bundle, of barley or wheat. One bundle was brought to the Temple every day for the fifty days between Pesaḥ and Shavuot.

פֶּסַח **Pesaḥ,** Passover, is the spring holiday of matzah and of freedom. It celebrates the deliverance of the Hebrews from Egyptian slavery.

פִּדְיוֹן הַבֵּן **Pidyon ha-Ben,** redemption of the first-born son, a ceremony held thirty days after the birth.

פּוּרִים **Purim,** the Feast of Lots, the holiday celebrating the saving of the Jews of Persia by Esther and Mordecai.

רֹאשׁ הַשָּׁנָה **Rosh Hashanah,** the holiday marking the New Year.

רֹאשׁ הַשָּׁנָה לְאִילָנוֹת **Rosh Hashanah Leilanot,** the New Year of the Trees. See **Tu bi-Shevat.**

רֹאשׁ חֹדֶשׁ **Rosh Ḥodesh,** the first day of the Hebrew month.

Seder, "order," refers to the ceremony, and the meal that is part of the ceremony, opening the Pesaḥ festival. See **Pesaḥ.** סֵדֶר

Sefirah, "counting," are the days of the counting of the Omer. סְפִירָה

Shabbat ha-Gadol, the "great" Sabbath, is the one preceding Pesaḥ. שַׁבָּת הַגָּדוֹל

Shabbat Shalom, the Shabbat greeting, "the peace of the Sabbath." שַׁבָּת שָׁלוֹם

Shabbat Shuvah, "Shabbat of Return," the Sabbath that falls between Rosh Hashanah and Yom Kippur. שַׁבָּת שׁוּבָה

Shaddai, one of the names by which Jews refer to God. שַׁדַּי

Shaḥarit, morning, refers to the morning service. שַׁחֲרִית

Shalaḥ-manot, gifts, generally food, given to friends and neighbors during Purim. See **Purim.** שָׁלַח מָנוֹת

Shavua Tov, "good week," is a greeting said after the Shabbat. שָׁבוּעַ טוֹב

Shavuot, the harvest festival that comes seven weeks after Pesaḥ. It also celebrates the giving of the Torah at Mount Sinai. שָׁבוּעוֹת

Shel Rosh, the *Tefillin* placed on the forehead. See **Tefillin.** שֶׁל־רֹאשׁ

Shel Yad, the *Tefillin* worn on the arm. See **Tefillin.** שֶׁל־יָד

Shema, "hear," is the opening word, and the name, of the basic Jewish prayer. It comes from the Bible, Deuteronomy 6:4-9. שְׁמַע

Shemini Atzeret, the eighth day of the Sukkot holiday. See **Sukkot.** שְׁמִינִי עֲצֶרֶת

Shem Tov, a good name. שֵׁם טוֹב

Shivah, "seven," refers to the seven days of deep mourning following the death of a member of the immediate family. שִׁבְעָה

Shofar, the ram's horn that was the signal and warning horn of the ancient Hebrews. It is a commandment to sound the shofar on Rosh Hashanah. שׁוֹפָר

Simḥat Torah, the "rejoicing of the Torah," is the happy day when the year-long cycle of reading the Torah ends, and the next cycle begins. שִׂמְחַת תּוֹרָה

Sukkot, the fall harvest festival named for the *sukkah,* or hut, in which the harvesters lived during the gathering of the fruits. סֻכּוֹת

Tefillin, the square boxes worn on the forehead *(Shel Rosh)* and upper arm *(Shel Yad)* during morning prayers on weekdays. Inside the boxes are parchments with verses from the Torah. תְּפִלִּין

Tisha be-Av, the ninth day of the month of Av, a fast day marking the destruction of the Temple. תִּשְׁעָה בְּאָב

Torah, the first of the three parts of the *Tanakh,* the Bible. The Torah contains the first five books of the Bible known as the books of Moses. It is written on a scroll and kept in the Ark in the synagogue. The books of the Torah are: *Bereshit, Shemot, Vayikra, Bamidbar, Devarim.* תּוֹרָה

Tu bi-Shevat, the 15th day of the month of Shevat, the day on which the New Year of the Trees is celebrated. ט״ו בִּשְׁבָט

Tzedakah, "righteousness," has come to mean acts of righteousness or of charity. צְדָקָה

Yamim Noraim, the Days of Awe, the ten days that begin with Rosh Hashanah and end with Yom Kippur. יָמִים נוֹרָאִים

Yizkor, "remember," refers to the service of remembrance for the dead. יִזְכּוֹר

Yom Kippur, the solemn Day of Atonement. יוֹם כִּפּוּר

Index

Abraham, 20, 23, 30, 46, 55, 63, 147, 169, 218, 227
Afikoman, 126, 127, 130
Ahad Ha-Am, 87
Ahasuerus, 191
Akiva, Rabbi, 102, 136, 138
Alénu, 226
Al Ḥet, 238, 239, 240
Antiochus, 173, 174, 176, 180, 181
Ark, 38, 43, 79, 177, 178, 205, 236
Avodah, 241

Baal Shem Tov, 11
Babylon, 30, 87, 88, 112, 153, 200
Bar Kokhba, 136, 180, 203
Bar Mitzvah, 14, 16, 39, 40, 41, 42, 43, 64, 96, 100, 149, 163, 165
Bat Mitzvah, 14, 16, 39, 40, 41, 42, 43, 64, 148
Berit Milah, 22, 25, 64
Besamim, 96
Betrothal, 48, 49, 51
Betzah, 123, 124
Bimah, 38, 51, 157, 165
Bitter herbs, 121, 123, 130
Bokser, 186
Burial, 71, 72

Circumcision, 20, 21, 22, 23, 24, 25, 28, 85, 173
Commandment, 21, 24, 39, 41, 57, 59, 79, 123, 130, 140, 153, 154, 156, 159, 173, 212, 213, 234, 235, 238, 246
Confirmation, 16, 43, 148, 149
Covenant, 20, 22, 23, 24, 85, 173, 200, 225, 233

Dayenu, 129
Day of Atonement, 233, 237
Days of Awe, 79, 209, 210, 215, 216, 217, 241, 243
Death, 67, 68, 70, 71, 72, 75, 77, 78, 79
Dietary laws, 60, 62
Dreidel, 179, 180

Ecclesiastes, 195
Elijah, 22, 24, 30, 54, 121, 123, 130, 131
End of Days, 9, 10, 43, 246, 248, 250
Eshet Ḥayil, 91
Esther, 190, 191, 192, 194, 195, 198
Eternal Light, 178

Etrog, 154, 155, 156, 157, 158
Etz Ḥayyim, 182
Exodus, 152, 169, 199

Fasts, 79, 201, 202, 204, 206, 233, 234, 235, 2
Fast of Esther, 194, 202
Fast of Gedaliah, 216
Federation of Jewish Philanthropies, 197
Festival of Freedom, 117, 127
First Temple, 30, 87, 88, 206
Four Questions, 127, 129
Funeral, 64, 68, 70, 72, 73, 75

Geshem, 158
Grager, 195

Haftarah, 121, 205, 216, 240, 241
Haggadah, 120, 121, 123, 124
Ḥag ha-Bikkurim, 143
Ha-Gomel, 96
Hakkafot, 163
Ḥallah (ḥallot), 91, 93, 94, 222
Haman, 191, 192, 195, 196
Hamantaschen, 234
Ḥametz, 123, 153
Ḥamishah Asar bi-Shevat, 115, 184
Ḥanukkah, 20, 32, 57, 64, 105, 106, 171, 17 174, 175, 176, 177, 178, 179, 180, 181, 18 249
Ḥaroset, 123, 130
Ḥasidism, 11, 163
Hasmonean, 175, 176
Ḥatan Bereshit, 165
Ḥatan Torah, 163
Havdalah, 64, 96
Ḥevrah Kaddisha, 71
Hillel, 30, 130, 178
Hoshana Rabbah, 158
Ḥupah, 52, 185

Isaiah, 182, 187, 192, 205, 240
Israel Independence Day, 139

Jerusalem, 87, 144, 145, 153, 171, 181, 186, 18 196, 200, 202, 203, 204, 241
Jewish National Fund, 187
Johanan ben Zakkai, 184
Jubilee year, 247, 248
Judah Ha-Nasi, 204

addish, 74, 76
arpas, 123, 125, 126
ashrut, 60, 61, 62
etubah, 51, 53, 54
ibbutzim, 159
iddush, 93, 94, 125, 154, 222, 235
iddush cup, 64, 91
ddushin, 46
ohen, Kohanim, 26, 124
ol Nidre, 235, 236, 237, 238, 240
osher, 223

ag ba-Omer, 132, 133, 135, 136, 137, 138, 139
amb bone, 123, 124
amentations, 195, 205
vites, 145, 174
ulav, 154, 155, 156, 157, 158

a'ariv, 102
accabee, Judah, 171, 174, 180
accabees, 20, 36, 105, 120, 173, 175, 181
aimonides, 36, 212, 213, 246
anna, 91
aot hittim, 122, 186
aror, 123, 130
arriage, 13, 14, 20, 24, 41, 44, 45, 46, 48, 49, 51, 54, 55, 135
asada, 226
attathias, 171, 172, 173, 174, 175
atzah, 122, 123, 124, 126, 127, 130, 131, 153
atzevah, 76
egillah, 195
enorah, 20, 64, 176, 177, 178, 179, 181
essiah, 24, 70, 131, 148, 184, 205
essiah, Days of, 9, 14, 25, 34, 46, 79, 81, 97, 103, 131, 198, 225, 228, 244, 246, 250
ezuzah, 59, 60, 63
idrash, 129, 155, 215, 239
inhah, 102
nyan, 76
ishnah, 115, 144, 204
itzvah (mitzvot), 21, 24, 25, 39, 71, 75, 76, 101, 230, 235, 248, 249
izrah, 64
odin, 171, 172, 173
ohel, 22, 24, 28
ordecai, 190, 191, 198
oses, 142, 146, 147
otzi, 79, 125, 130, 222, 235
ount Sinai, 41, 142, 146, 147, 225
ourning, 72, 74, 75, 76

azis, 121, 131, 187, 198, 241
ilah, 242, 243
er Tamid, 178

New Year, 14, 64, 151, 210, 211, 216, 219, 220, 227, 228
New Year of the Trees, 115, 184, 185, 187, 188

Omer, 132, 133, 134, 135, 136, 137, 138, 139, 143

Palestine, 157, 186, 194
Passover, 117, 121, 122, 123, 124, 129, 130, 168
Pesah, 21, 32, 54, 57, 64, 77, 86, 106, 109, 110, 113, 117, 118, 119, 121, 122, 123, 126, 129, 131, 132, 133, 134, 135, 143, 151, 152, 160, 177, 178, 186, 191, 195, 234, 249
Pharaoh, 118, 119, 130, 146
Phylacteries, 99
Pidyon ha-Ben, 25
Pirké Avot, 95
Plagues, 118, 129
Promised Land, 151, 159, 169
Purim, 64, 177, 190, 191, 192, 193, 194, 195, 196, 197, 198, 234

Redemption of the first-born, 25
Roasted egg, 123, 124
Rosh Hashanah, 14, 76, 86, 106, 110, 112, 113, 114, 115, 210, 211, 215, 216, 218, 219, 220, 221, 222, 223, 225, 226, 227, 228, 242, 249
Rosh Hodesh, 113, 114
Ruth, 148, 195

Sabbath, 22, 24, 28, 51, 55, 65, 77, 87, 93, 98, 103, 110, 111, 140, 146, 210; *see* Shabbat
Sabbatical year, 247, 248
Sanhedrin, 135
Sayings of the Fathers, 95
Sea of Reeds, 119, 129
Second Temple, 30, 88, 135, 206, 230
Seder, 56, 64, 119, 120, 121, 122, 123, 124, 125, 126, 127, 130, 131, 146, 153, 234
Seder plate, 64, 123
Sefirah, 132, 135, 136, 137
Shabbat, 64, 83, 85, 86, 87, 88, 89, 90, 91, 93, 94, 95, 96, 97, 100, 111, 113, 114, 121, 157, 161, 173, 205, 209, 216, 220, 225, 230, 248; *see* Sabbath
Shabbat ha-Gadol, 121
Shabbat Shuvah, 216
Shaharit, 99, 102
Shalah-manot, 196
Shammai, 175
Shammash, 178, 179
Shavuot, 43, 54, 57, 77, 86, 106, 109, 113, 132, 133, 134, 135, 142, 143, 144, 145, 146, 147, 148, 149, 151, 152, 153, 160, 168, 178, 195
Sheheheyanu, 20, 23, 223

Shel Rosh, 100
Shel Yad, 100
Shem Tov, 34
Shema, 38, 41, 59, 71, 102, 231, 243
Shemini Atzeret, 157, 158, 159, 161
Shivah, 75, 76
Shofar, 113, 223, 225, 226, 243
Shushan, 194
Simeon ben Yoḥai, 136, 137, 138, 139
Simḥah, 188
Simḥat Torah, 14, 38, 157, 161, 162, 163, 165, 167, 169
Song of Songs, 195
Spice box, 64, 96
Sukkah, 56, 152, 154, 158, 234
Sukkot, 57, 64, 77, 86, 109, 113, 151, 152, 153, 154, 155, 156, 157, 158, 159, 160, 169, 176, 178, 195, 234

Tallit, 52, 99, 165
Talmud, 17, 25, 28, 36, 40, 41, 45, 50, 52, 60, 65, 70, 75, 89, 106, 176, 183, 185, 206, 225, 230
Tashlich, 227
Tefillin, 40, 99, 100, 205
Ten Commandments, 48, 86, 148, 153, 154
Ten Days of Repentance, 211, 215, 243
Teshuvah, 216
Tisha be-Av, 32, 54, 195, 202, 203, 204, 205, 206, 207, 233

Torah, 10, 14, 18, 19, 20, 25, 28, 29, 36, 40, 41, 43, 46, 51, 62, 68, 74, 81, 86, 95, 100, 102, 114, 115, 120, 124, 133, 139, 1 143, 145, 146, 147, 148, 149, 152, 155, 1 162, 163, 165, 166, 167, 173, 182, 184, 1 199, 205, 221, 231, 235, 236, 240, 241, 2
Tu bi-Shevat, 115, 184, 185, 186, 187, 188,
Tzaddik, 11
Tzedakah, 202

Unleavened bread, 117, 119, 120, 123

Vashti, 191
Viddui, 238

Western Wall, 204

Yahrzeit, 77
Yamim Noraim, 209
Yizkor, 77, 158, 241
Yom Kippur, 22, 77, 79, 83, 86, 99, 110, 1 202, 206, 210, 211, 213, 216, 219, 226, 2 230, 231, 232, 233, 234, 235, 236, 238, 2 240, 241, 242, 243, 247, 249
Yom Tov, 32

Zemirot, 95
Zeroa, 123, 124
Zohar, 14